The View From Here
Vile Knowledge

by

Barbara J. Knutsen

Barbara J. Knutsen
P.O Box 1217
Tolleson, AZ 85353
www.barbaraj.knutsen.com

Printed in the United States of America
First Printing December 2009
ISBN: 978-0-578-04956-4
Barbara J. Knutsen

Drawings by Barbara J. Knutsen while in counseling
Photos are the property of Barbara J. Knutsen
Cover Design and Typesetting: C. J. Lovell
Editing: C. J. Lovell
Graphics: Dana Sitarzewski / Jaguar Woman Web Design
www.jaguarwoman.com

Dedication

To those victims of incest and other forms of sexual abuse who sincerely want to become survivors, put their negative pasts behind them, and get on with the life God intended them to have.

Acknowledgments

Neither this book nor my recovery would have been possible without the steadfast love, patience, and constant support of my husband, Allan, who allowed me to feel safe to relive through memories my dark past; or the counseling of my therapist, Ron Bell. Heartfelt thanks to my daughters, grandchildren, and understanding friends who gave me comfort and helped me know and accept that I am worthy of non-abusive love; also, to the spiritual counselors who helped me cleanse my mind of evil lies I was told about my Lord and Savior. And above all, my ever-lasting gratitude to God, who guided me through every step of the recovery process.

Author's Notes

As you will see so graphically in Part 1: The View From Here, Vile Knowledge; before the age of six, I was preconditioned to tolerate verbal, physical, emotional, mental, and sexual abuse.

The tortures I survived at the hands of a cousin affected my personality and pre-set a future of repeated abuse spanning over three decades.

I did not talk -- could not talk -- about the cesspool of experiences that were a sickening memory frozen deep inside.

There were lies I believed and truths that terrified me.

Finally, unable to live with those lies and secrets any longer, the frozen cubicles of repressed anger, terror, humility, guilt, loneliness, and denial began to melt as I faced a torrent of horrifying memories. I accepted that I needed extensive therapy and grabbed hold of the belief that it was vital for recovery.

Faith in God and His promises saved my soul and gave me inner peace and the courage to face the truth about my past.

Healing is taking place in my body, mind, and sprit.

My fervent hope and prayer is that this book will help others who are holding on to another person's lies, shame, and secrets and enable them to find the faith and confidence to face the truth that will set them free.

I also pray this book will make a major difference in getting society to refuse to tolerate incestuous abuse so the children presently being victimized can have hope for their pain to end as mine has -- only much sooner.

Barbara Knutsen

Prologue

Blood vessels throbbed in my head. Sweat beaded on my face.

Again!

The odor of feces was overwhelming. This went on for three months; into what would become five years of therapy.

The first such experience surfaced while I was watching on TV the Clarence Thomas and Anita Hill proceedings before the United States Senate. As Hill remarked about Thomas, saying something about his "Long John Dong," a voice in the back of my head said, "They'd never put on TV what happened to me."

The voice was so loud and clear that I looked to see if someone was in the room with me. Moments later I heard the voice again – now well aware that it came from inside my head – saying, "No one would believe what happened to me, no less on TV."

The smell of feces was sudden and growing suffocatingly strong. Anxiety engulfed me. Paranoia set in.

The diagnosis was 'Post Trauma Syndrome'.

Then the counseling began.

Memories thawed and flowed.

Table of Contents

Part 1 – The Numbness of Nowhere

I walk, smile and say, "I'm feeling great!"
It's all a lie.

As truth has it,
I'm hanging on by a thin thread of faith.

In reality,
I'm hiding my pain as no one cares to know.

I'm a breath away from heaven, an eternity away from affection,
Caught in this hallow place, between here and there.

'The Numbness of Nowhere'

The Set-Up

Although sexually abused by both Mom and Dad before age five, the real nightmare lay ahead. It began to unfold during Christmas holiday, 1950, at a relative's house not far from where we lived in Ramsey, New Jersey.

The night air was crisp and clean smelling; snow sparkled in the moonlight as we drove to a Christmas party at Sue and Lou's house in Midland Park, New Jersey.

Sue and Lou lived in a two story hillside house on E. Summit Street about 100 feet from the road; an upper class neighborhood in Midland Park, just off Prospect Street. They were wealthy; had very nice furniture and wore the finest clothes.

Sue was a buxom woman a bit on the heavy side and wore glasses. Her face reminded me of a Pekinese, flat, wide and round.

I didn't like going to Sue and Lou's house. She would stare at me with scornful eyes; and there was never a smile on her face. I felt deeply she didn't like children.

Sixty-year-old Sue, much older sister to my father, Sid Zeister, was one spiteful woman who had ways of not only getting mad, but even. What she had against my mother, Martha, my five-and-a-half-year-old mind could not fathom.

I was playing carefree and minding my own business when Sue distracted me. "Go find your mommy, down the hall in the back bedroom," she said. Obediently, naively, I walked to that particular bedroom and opened the door. The bedroom was dark. I heard moaning noises as I stood quietly in the doorway. They did not notice me right away. Harry, my thirty-year-old cousin and nephew to my father, was gyrating on top of Mother in the guest bed. I thought they were wrestling or tickling each other. When they realized I had "caught them in the act," they were angry, shocked and scared. Their facial expressions caused me to think I was "naughty" for having seen them.

Even as I began to bolt from the bedroom doorway, Mom was getting off the bed to quickly tidy herself. I ran outside and found Dad in the back yard smoking, drinking a beer and talking with the other men at the party. I tried to tell him about what I had seen, but, he was too drunk to listen. He kept pushing me away; telling me to go play. Mom rushed out and grabbed hold of me. She gave me her evil-eyed look that meant STIFLE!

Mom took me back in the house where all the wives were gossiping and talking about various things. I wasn't allowed to leave my mother's side the rest of the evening. I sat next to her "fidgeting" and "squirming" with boredom, but knew better not to move from that spot.

Harry and Mother were terrified to the point of paranoia.

In the few months that followed, Mom told Harry she was growing weary of intervening in my attempts to tell. They were so afraid I might blab about their affair to Dad they made plans to make sure beyond any possible doubt that I would keep my little mouth shut.

No way on God's green earth could I have ever imagined that before summer I would escape death by burial, near-drowning, and hanging; and witness a murder.

Harry's mother died when he was about three. His dad and older brothers raised him. Relatives have told me that Harry was abused as a child and grew up cold hearted without his mother's love. World War II enabled Harry to learn vicious torture techniques. He returned from his tour in Italy an angry, bitter person known to torture animals and children. Harry's cousin Johnny told me Harry had sex with animals. He was a full blown alcoholic; a mean and nasty drunk and was ostracized by most of the relatives.

Mom and Harry's fear drove them to put a plan on the burner that came to a boil one night in April, 1950. Harry and his wife, Amy visited our home. Harry was approximately six foot, medium build with sandy brown hair. He resembled Oswald, (*the man that shot Kennedy*). His eyes were deep and dark looking. His eyes and face were full of hate. I was scared when he looked at me.

Harry and my dad drank a lot of beer when Harry and his family came to visit. .

Dad stood six-feet-one-inch tall; had broad shoulders, platinum sandy blond hair and sky blue eyes. Both Harry and my dad were hot tempered and fought when they drank.

It was really quite a simple plot. Harry downed several beers and badgered Dad into a fight. In the middle of the brawl, Mom called the police.

Although Harry had started things, Dad was the one arrested for assault and battery, and hauled off to jail. I remember hating the policemen for taking my dad off to jail and not even asking who was to blame for the fight.

What ensued was a week I will always remember as 'Horrors from Hell.'

The following day, Mother took me to Harry's house; said I was going to stay with Aunt Amy while she went shopping. I got out of the car. She closed and locked the door behind me and did not get out. She told Harry, "Do NOT leave any marks I can't hide with clothes and shoes."

Fear owned every muscle of my body. Tears welled up and I begged Mom not to leave me there. She ignored my cries and started to drive off. I ran screaming after the car, but both Mom and the vehicle were quickly out of sight. Standing about three feet from Harry, I was scared and felt abandoned.

Amy, hearing my cries came out of the house, beckoned to me and calmed me down. "Your momma will be back soon. Just don't you worry."

I was a skinny cute little kid, about 4 foot tall, hazel green eyes, with chestnut brown natural curly hair that went to my shoulders. It was a chilly April morning. I wore a long sleeve dress with a sweater over top. I looked down at my black pattent shoes; stared at them feeling alone and angry my mom left me there and wished my sister Doris Lee were there with me. I was four years younger than my sister Doris Lee who was about nine years' old attending grade school. Step-sisters, Mary and Tish both attended high school at the time.

I stood pouting, not knowing how long it would be before my mom would come to pick me up.

Season Ticket Holders

Harry and Amy's house was in a small town of Oakland, New Jersey, not far from Ramsey. It was deep in the woods at the base of the Ramapo Mountains. It was very isolated, far from any neighbors, making it a perfect location to commit unspeakable and criminal acts.

Harry had two brothers; John and Bob. They had custom built homes located in an upper class neighborhood in Wyckoff, a few towns away.

Harry's house was in a poor area in Oakland; a small weathered drab olive green oblong trailer shaped house. It had two small bedrooms, a small living room with a fire place, one bathroom, a small kitchen, plus a porch area Amy used as a beauty polar.

Amy was a lousy house keeper. There wasn't an empty space on the kitchen counters and the sink was always full of dirty dishes. The kitchen had worn out linoleum flooring. The rest of the house had old wood floors covered with throw rugs here and there. In the living room stood Harry's high back overstuffed chair which sat next to a small couch and small TV.

The living room was not well lit; full of old news papers and lots of "stuff" jammed into the corners.

The kid's bedroom was small with two twin beds and a small closet. Harry and Amy's double bed and dresser was all they could fit in their small bedroom.

While Amy piled the supper dishes in the sink, I played Sunday school with Harry and Amy's two kids, Lynn Sue, seven and Roy, four. Lynn Sue stood about five feet; not very pretty in the face, but she had gentle eyes and was quiet, humble, kind and always submissive to Harry's commands.

Roy stood about three and a half feet tall, short legs and a long torso. He had a "taunting" brat personality. His eyes looked angry and sad at the same time. He was always the cause of Lynn Sue getting whippings. When I tried to be nice to him, he would bite me, so I kept my distance.

I remember my mother saying she would like to smother Roy with a pillow if she knew she could get away with it.

Harry, meanwhile, was sitting in his overstuffed high back chair, downing one beer after another, building up his courage.

I was in Lynn Sue's bedroom. We were playing Sunday school. Lynn Sue and I both had dresses on. We were singing "Jesus Loves Me" when Harry barged in and jerked me up by my arm and stripped me of my clothing. It happened so fast, I immediately felt fear pounding in my head and heart. I saw Lynn Sue and Roy back up with a look of fear on their faces. They stood silent.

Harry was raging, spewing forth angry vile obscenities and opinions on things I knew nothing about. To say I was scared would be a terrible understatement. I was yelling and screaming while terror and confusion consumed me.

"Amy!" Harry screeched. "Get your butt in here!" She rushed into the room. Harry's glassy-eyed stare nearly stapled wife, son and daughter to the wall. The three of them went into a deep silence and fell into their roles like season ticket holders.

It was as if Harry could not hear my screams. His eyes were bloodshot, red and evil looking. The purple veins on his face were bulging like worms under his skin. He wore tan khaki work pants, an unbuttoned plaid shirt exposing his hairy chest. His mannerisms were reminiscent of the devil as he threw me onto the bed. I was absolutely horrified.

He turned me on my back, stretched my flexible little legs over my head, used spit to saturate his finger and began probing my rectum as though it were a pliable toy. Pants already unbuttoned, he rubbed spit on his erect penis and thrust it into my rectum, into the depths of self-satisfaction.

The excruciating pain was more than I could endure as Harry followed thrust with thrust. My mind froze the experience in time. I seemed to leave my body. The smell of my own feces repeatedly brought me out of the numbness of nowhere.

He pulled me into a sitting position on the edge of the bed, grabbed my head, and forced his feces-coated penis into my mouth. The faster and deeper he penetrated my throat, the more I disassociated and gagged. I nearly suffocated from my own feces which Harry then smeared on my teeth, down the back of my throat, up my nose, and into my eyes and hair.

Harry said I smelled like the pile of shit I was, "just like your old man", my dad.

With his penis inches past my glottis, he finally ejaculated, acting like he was worshipping something deep inside himself.

He forced me to swallow what he called "seeds of knowledge."

Then, with his face almost touching mine and his wretched breath reeking with alcohol and stale cigarettes, he arrogantly said, "Where's your Jesus now?"

Wounded, confused, frightened, crying, and spiritually shattered, I watched Harry leave the room. Amy finally moved away from the wall. She took me to the bathroom to clean me up and all the while I could think of nothing else but telling my daddy. But Harry had plans to assure I would not do that.

I was still in the tub when he staggered into the bathroom with another beer in his hand. He glared at Amy. "Give her to me! I haven't even started to teach her to keep her little nose out of other peoples' business!"

From that moment and for the following five days and nights he kept me naked and terrified while he inflicted unspeakable acts upon and into my young, tender body and innocent mind.

This took place during a brisk April in 1950.

AUTHOR'S COMMENT: Before and during my five years of counseling I wrote poems as a way of expressing past hurts and inching toward recovery. Some of those poems are presented in this book.

According to Lust

According to lust, she's always to blame,
She made it hard, that's why he came.

According to lust, he's not responsible for his acts,
That's about the time he says, "JUST RELAX".

According to lust, she's asking for it,
Says the voice inside his head,
Justifying his next move, as he throws her on the bed.

According to lust, it's because she's so pretty,
The way she smells,
Her dress, those hugs, the sexy way she walks and talks,
The way she bats her beautiful eyes,
Her butt, how it connects just right to her thighs.

"It would be a pity to pass that all by"- according to lust.

Hot tempered, he decided to make her his toy,
When she was most confident and so full of joy.

Or was it when she was emotionally off guard?

It was when "he" desired, according to "his" rules,

Which were vicious, crude and rude.
His words were ambiguous,
Did he mean what she heard, did she hear what he said?

"Fuck me, suck me, if you don't you're dead."

According to lust, his accountability was totally blocked out,
Giving him reason to holler and shout,

"Guess what's next on my list,
Don't move an inch or I'll bust ya with my fist!"

According to lust, it was time for the ultimate experience,
Doing what he loved best,
Having sex with an unconsenting child.

Crated

That first night Harry locked my naked little body in a wooden crate outside in his back yard, telling me, "I keep all my shit outside". I coiled into a fetal position trying to fend off the chill. But, my bones soon began to ache from the cold and wind. It felt like it was going to snow. It was a night of shivering and whimpering like an abandoned puppy. The only comfort I remember receiving was from the family dog, a black and tan German shepherd. He curled up against the crate, panted his warm breath onto my face and blocked some of the cold air hitting me. Drifting in and out of numbness, I wept wondering WHY?

Like a ritual, just before dawn every morning, the porch light came on. Harry stepped out, dressed the same each day, holding a coffee cup in hand. He'd pull a match across a dark patch on the wall next to the back door and lit a cigarette already crimped between his lips. And again the torture began.

Although convinced that I must have done something really bad to be forced to endure such pain, I could not figure out what it could have been.

Harry performed on me what seemed like a never-ending barrage of horrifying experiments and self-gratifying indulgences. First, he tied me down by my wrists and ankles to a work bench in his shed. The wooden shed was old; located about 20 feet behind Harry's house. It had a work bench at one end and tools of all sorts sitting against the walls. He put a small block of ice on my tummy and left it there until it burned like a branding iron. The skin on my tummy didn't have any feeling, it just burned. He shoved one earthworm after another up my left nostril and eagerly enjoyed watching my agony of being repulsed as they crawled down the back of my throat causing me to gag and vomit. Harry then forced me to eat that vomit until I learned not to throw it up. It had an acidy taste that burned my throat as I swallowed it over and over. My regular diet during that week of hell was raw vegetables, raw fish scraps, canned dog food, and an occasional chocolate bar that Amy would sneak out to me. "It will keep your energy up," she said.

Harry gave me enemas using a variety of fluids. Car oil, castor oil, hot coffee, beer, gasoline mixed with milk, pet and people urine. I was acutely nauseated from these substances which burned my insides, made me sweat profusely, and gave me atrocious gas, cramps, and convulsive reactions. I could see him sneering with a smile on his face as though it made him feel good to see me suffer as I continued to wonder, WHY?

The more I fought him, the more he tortured me. He gave me soapy enemas, followed by more sodomy. Once he rubbed something on my bottom and manipulated his German shepherd dog into sodomizing me. He convinced my naive mind that I would soon be pooping puppies. My intestines were bellowing with pain and I was fretting with horror. I actually began to believe that live puppies were growing inside my rectum.

Boredom set in and Harry went beyond what he considered trivial torture. He attached an electrical wire to one end of a steel rod. He inserted the other end of the rod into my rectum and gave me "electrical shock treatments." My body felt like it was vibrating from inside. Repeated shocks caused me to temporarily lose my vision. This petrified me and shook Harry. I remember being blind for what seemed like hours before regaining my sight. After that, Harry set a limit on the amount of electrical shock I received, yet he still administered it whenever the mood struck him.

He inserted a needle into my back through my ribs and it felt like it went into my left lung. This was very painful and made me feel like a lab rat. I began to wonder if I was going to die.

Harry caught a baby mouse; greased it with axle grease and forced the live "itty bitty" mouse into my rectum and delighted in my contortions as it squirmed and tried to burrow its way out. I lost touch with reality during this torture, became delirious, and felt very sick.

He put black slimy leeches on my back and arms; told me they would suck the poison from my soul. He put a copper tube up my rectum, and then blew air into it until my tummy was painfully extended. I felt like my intestines were going to explode. After what seemed like forever, he released the air rumbling inside me. The force of the backed-up air created an exuberantly loud bellowing sound. Harry sang out, "Gabriel, come blow your horn!" Then, in an almost guttural rasp, he said, "I bet your God is proud of you now."

He also used a bike pump, inserting it into my rectum to bloat my tummy with air just to hear me pass loud gas and laugh at me.   Humiliation, anger, pain, shame, guilt and extreme sadness overwhelmed me.

One night while I was locked in the crate, a large brown bear came out of the nearby Ramapo Mountains. As it neared the crate I was in, the bear growled and showed its huge white teeth and dark tongue. It busted the crate open, grabbed my arm, and began to drag me away. The noise of the bear growling and my screams awakened Harry. Soon I heard a combination of the bear growling, Harry yelling, and a shot from his rifle.

Wounded, the bear let go of me and lumbered off.

Vile Knowledge

In a snake pit, consumed in fear; waiting for its bite.
Death comes not, and leaves me here, in pain to wonder.

Suddenly, one crawls inside me, entering through my nostril,
Forcing me to swallow.

Once ingested, the bile quickly eats away,
Deteriorating its flesh.

Have I just been nourished?
No, only compelled to vomit, to eat it once again,
Until it becomes a part of me and readies me for more.

"Vile Knowledge"

Message from God

Harry picked up my naked, aching body, tied my hands behind my back, and tied my ankles together. "You're causing me more trouble than you're worth," he said. I still couldn't figure out WHY?

My new quarters was a large milk can into which he stuffed me and fastened the lid. His sinister voice sent shivers through me. I could hear him clearly even though the lid was in place. "Sleep tight, don't let the spiders and bugs bite. Ha! Ha! Ha!" His laugh echoed with power and control which aroused a growing anger within me. Yet, I began to feel that I was evil while being held captive in my helpless and hopeless condition.

The few hours left of total darkness dragged.

It was already daylight before Harry reappeared. He removed the lid and said, "I brought you some company." He dropped a large black-and-red snake on me and quickly closed the lid. Harry laughed when I shrieked in horror. But this time, thank God, he didn't hang around.

I quivered and squealed as the snake crawled and wrapped its body around me and eventually came to rest its head upon my chest. I calmed down as I began to hear an inner-realm voice speak to me. To this day, I believe that was my first encounter with God. Deep inside, I somehow knew that it was God talking to me through the snake. I heard Him say He was my friend; that I would be okay, and to listen to what He said.

The snake and I spent the entire day and night in that milk can, and I listened while He enlightened me. He said Harry was sick and listened to the devil. He told me to love my enemies no matter what and assured me he would stay with me and protect me always. I wondered why God didn't stop Harry and didn't rescue me.

Almost Drowned, Buried Alive, Hanged

The lull of almost peacefulness ended abruptly. The next morning, Harry removed me from the milk can, took me to a nearby pond and plunged me head first into it. The water was ice cold. He held me under until I began to take in water. He pulled me up and I'd grab and choke for air. He did this over and over until I lost all resistance to struggle. I felt a darkness coming over me and lost consciousness during this ordeal.

On the drive back to the shed at Harry's house, he was laughing as he told me, "That was your first swimming lesson." Over four decades later I am still terrified of the water.

Once back in his torture shed, Harry built a box "just your size," he said. It was about four feet long, one-and-a-half feet wide, and one-foot high. He taped my mouth shut, tied my hands and feet, laid me face up in the box, nailed the lid on, and buried me in a hole, just inches deeper than the box was high. I heard the sound of what sounded like him putting plastic over the box. I could hear him singing, "The worms crawl in, the worms crawl out... you're on your way to meet God." I could see daylight between the pieces of wood. Then I heard the sound of dirt being shoveled onto the box and it got very dark. My muffled screams made my heart pound all the more. As I struggled, terror seemed to rob me of my breath. I soiled myself with excretion. My mind went into a state of delirium. Soon, I felt my brain and heart pulsing toward an explosion from lack of oxygen.

I don't know how long I had been buried when the frantic sounds of someone scraping off the dirt and plastic jolted me alert. The lid was pried off.

It was Amy. As she lifted me from the box and removed the tape from my mouth, I was both relieved and mortified. I was glad to be out of the coffin and held in human arms, yet, I feared what Harry would do to me next. Each time I thought it was over, he would think of something else to subject me to.

Harry had told me, "I am trying to teach you something that you are too stupid to understand." I remember thinking, "If I am too stupid to understand, will I never learn, will it ever stop?"

Amy pleaded for him to stop torturing me. "What has this child done to you? Why are you doing this?"

"Quit your meddling, woman!" Harry warned Amy as we approached the house.

In a flash Harry jerked me from Amy's arms and pulled me close to his face. His alcohol-stanched breath swept over me as he said, "You love Niggers so much little girl. *(My family was close to an African American family named Houston, and I was very close to Grandmother Houston.)* You know what we do to nigger lovers, don't you?"

He quickly scrambled, still clutching me close to his chest into the house where he found a sheet. Back outside, he used the sheet to hang me from a tree limb. He and Amy watched as I jerked, squirmed, urinated and gagged for air. I had an orgasm, came face to face with God, and felt that I had literally left my painful little body. I believed I died. That was when I heard God speak to me again from that inner realm. I felt total peace, no pain, an unconditional love, that I was part of God as a whole. My eyes were so close to God's I could see forever. I saw God's Kingdom. It was pure white with gold in different places, winged angels walking around in TOTAL PEACE. God told me that I had to go back, He had plans for me, and He would be with me always. He said, as His servant, I would bring a multitude of wayward children back to his flock. I believe this book is a step in that direction.

The next thing I remember is being in Amy's arms, choking and coughing, while she rubbed my throat and begged Harry to quit before he killed me. "Sid would surely kill you if anything happened to his baby girl."

This did not stop Harry. Again he took me to his torture shed, tied me down, taped my mouth, and burned my left nipple with a cigarette. I passed out from the pain.

Next, he made me sit up and balance a metal object on my head. "This will build your character," he said. "Someone as bullish as you needs a strong neck and this ought to do it."

Throughout the week from hell, he repeatedly made me orally copulate him; swallow his sperm and consider it a meal.

Some evenings I was brought to the house and ordered to entertain the family by crawling on my hands and knees, pretending to be the family pet. Harry would make me lay under a lamp in the living room, masturbate with various objects, and keep at it until I reached an orgasm. Then he made me orally copulate Amy while he held the back of my head by the hair, shoving my face into her genitalia as though it were a halved watermelon. All this time, both Lynn Sue and Roy were ordered to watch.

Pretending To Be An Actress

What's my part, what's my line,
acting like me is all I know how to be.

What do I do?

("Pretend to be an actress")

Curtain's up, lights are on, the music's starting to play.

("That's your cue!")

The audience is waiting, the show's about to begin,
Her performance will earn spectacular reviews.

I'm not an observer without compassion,
I'm a witness; I was there, pretending to be an actress!

Between the things Harry said and what I was forced to do, I felt dirty, evil, and ashamed. I was too horrified and young to be able to really identify and describe what and how I was truly feeling, so I repressed my feelings, over and over, deeper and deeper into the numbness of nowhere.

Late one afternoon as I lay exhausted from a day's torture, I heard a car door close. Someone was coming into the shed. I twisted my head so I could see behind me. It was my mother! My mouth muffled by tape, I tried to scream and cry for her to help me. In synchronization with Harry, she told me, "Shut up!"

~ 38 ~

They talked about whether he had managed to teach me to keep my little mouth shut and whether or not to end their affair. "I've got a few more tricks up my sleeve," Harry said. "Give me a couple more days; she still has some fight left in her."

Mother nodded her consent, went to the car and drove away. Words could not describe the anger I felt at that moment. I was five-and-a-half, ripped completely apart, mentally, physically, and emotionally. The natural spiritual love that bonds a child to her mother was being peeled from my very soul. I felt totally abandoned and unloved. At this point, my self-esteem was totally destroyed.

I remembered what God told me about forgiving and not allowing evil to stop me from loving. I loved my mother until the day she passed away. I never grew to like her though. She wasn't a very nice person.

Harry removed the tape and untied me. He forced me to probe my anus and lick my feces-coated fingers and say, "Mmmmm what a good girl am I."

Days had already faded in and out of each other. He coated my tongue with bitters, told me I had just eaten poison and would soon begin to have convulsions and choke to death. Later, after laughing at my wide-eyed, mortified response, he said, "That was just some shit Amy uses to cook with. You will believe anything you're told."

The Murder

During the next-to-last day as Harry's prisoner, it was torture as usual in the shed. Only this time, Albin, watching from behind a tree, could see what Harry was doing.

Albin Loupawouski was a young retarded man who lived down the road. He said his dad was a police officer. Albin was approximately five-foot-eight-inches tall with blue eyes and dark brown hair. His eyes were set wide apart and he was slow minded, but always had a gentle smile and was very kind. I knew him and had trusted him. He periodically came to play with Lynn Sue and me. He would make small boats from leaves and sticks and we'd float them on the nearby pond. But that was during previous visits and before the event leading to my tortures. Times were very different now and Harry was really pissed when he noticed Albin.

Harry somehow mesmerized Albin and got him close enough to grab him. He pulled Albin's pants down and tried to sodomize him, but the boy got loose and began to run, yelling, "I'm gonna tell my momma!"

Amy came running out of the house screaming, "NO! NO! STOP!"

I was suddenly on the ground with Harry's foot on my chest. He had grabbed his deer rifle from inside the shed, and quickly aimed and fired. The bullet struck Albin in the back of his neck around his throat area. One moment the boy was running, the next he had dropped like a tall rock falling over with a thud. Still under Harry's foot; the sound of Albin's body hitting the ground rumbled like an echo into my body.

Amy was screaming like a mad woman. Harry slammed the rifle butt against her jaw, knocking her to the ground. "Shut your slant-eyed mouth before I shut it permanently!"

Amy was about five feet tall with long black hair. She was round faced; looked oriental. She obeyed Harry's every command. Amy was my rescuer and Harry's accomplice.

I was like petrified wood and knew by now not to make a sound. I held my screams inside my head where no one else could hear them, especially Harry. He dragged me over to Albin's body. "Now you will get a lesson you will never forget!"

He hanged Albin's body by the shirt collar from a spike on a tree. Then he got out a pocket knife and cut off the boy's ears and partially skinned his face. Bright red blood ran like water.

Gut-wrenching terror gripped me as I watched the torture master. Harry glanced at me and seemed pleased that I was frozen with fright.

He lowered Albin's body to the ground and I heard a gurgling sound as blood oozed from Albin's mouth. With the tip of the knife blade, Harry plucked out one of the boy's eyes and said, "The better to see you with, my dear." Then, he tore the boy's shirt open and grabbed an axe. Harry placed the axe handle between my hands, clamped his hands over mine, and with forceful blows we opened up the chest cavity. He reached in with his hand, cut off a piece of the boy's heart and made me eat it. It was still warm and had a rich blood taste. I felt very evil and lost. "The boy and you are now blood brothers," he said.

Harry then chopped off the very top of Albin's head and cut out matter to gross to describe, yet I knew it was brain. He made me eat some of that too. It was really bitter. Never have I tasted anything like it. "What you have just eaten and seen," Harry said, "is knowledge and is now part of you." I did not understand any of this. I thought it was the most evil thing there could possibly be and Harry was making me part of it.

Harry ordered me and Amy to dig a hole in which to bury Albin's body. Amy used a shovel. I used a trowel while Harry began mixing cement.

After Amy and I had dug a hole about four-feet deep, Harry called me over to the body. He again placed the axe handle in my hands and grasped my hands with his. We chopped off the fingers of Albin's right hand. Harry then put the body into the grave. He told me to pick up the finger pieces and place them where they belonged, at the ends of the finger stubs we had cut them from. Harry sang the Humpty Dumpty song.

This task done, he commanded me to do something sickeningly gruesome. Harry, Amy and their kids watched as I was forced to fornicate with the corpse until I reached a climax. Shame and humiliation overwhelmed me as I listened to his sacrilegious jargon. I seemed to be somewhere else at the time, out of my body again, in that place I had already come to know as "the numbness of nowhere."

Harry ordered me to stand up, started pouring in cement, and threatened to bury me alive with the corpse. My heart began to pound. I knew that he was capable of doing anything his evil mind conjured up. The cold, wet cement inched up my calves and past my knees. When I was neck deep, Harry put his face near mine and said, "Boo!!!" He roughly pulled me out of the grave of wet cement, held me by my upper arms and got nose to nose with me. His eyes were red and dark-circled, looking deep into mine. "If you ever tell anyone what you have seen... anything you have EVER seen ME do, I will do the same to you that I did to that retarded idiot. So you had better keep your little mouth shut, you hear?" (*Harry set in me a fear and destroyed my trust in all men. It took years of counseling and prayers to erase that mind-set.*)

Part of one more day was used up for torture and more of his self-satisfying indulgences, nothing he hadn't already done. While breaking for lunch, Harry got this look like he heard something in the distance. He shoved my taped-mouth, tied-up little body into the milk can, quickly secured the lid and told me not to make a sound, or ELSE!

Through a tiny hole in the side of the can I saw two police officers. I heard them question Harry about Albin, the missing retarded boy. "I haven't seen hide nor hair of him," Harry said.

The officers soon left, not having a clue that I was only a few feet away from them. Harry chuckled as they drove away. Rage engulfed me, tempered only by an equally strong feeling that I could not possibly be more alone. I felt God had abandoned me.

Albin's Heart & Hand with Fingers Cut

Harry placed the axe handle between my hands, clamped his hands over mine, and with forceful blows we opened up the chest cavity. He reached in with his hand, cut off a piece of the boy's heart and made me eat it. It was still warm and had a rich blood taste.

Suddenly

Suddenly, oh God, it's so final.
Now what?

Suddenly, oh God, face with no flesh.
Please don't!

Suddenly, oh dear God – please stop!

Picking up pieces, chop chop chop.

Suddenly, oh my God, tasting what beats no more.
What's next?

Suddenly, forcefully, lusting with death.
It's time?

Suddenly, pouring in the cement, burying the sin.
Pay attention!

Suddenly, hearing his threatening commands.
Blocking it all out.

Suddenly, lies and fear carry a lot of clout.

Sex Slave

Mom came for me just hours after Harry convinced police that he hadn't seen Albin. Only one thing was on her mind, and it had nothing to do with how much she missed me or how good it was to see me. "Did you learn to keep your little trap shut?" She asked as we drove away. There was no love in her eyes.

She questioned me all the way home. I passed the test because she didn't threaten to take me back to Harry's house right away. But, she held the threat constantly over me to keep me in line. And she didn't have to say anything, just give me that "LOOK" which horrified me.

Mom retrieved me from Harry within hours of Dad's return from jail. I believe Dad noticed a change in me, but didn't ask about anything that had happened to me while he was locked up. I felt he could see it in my eyes. I didn't dare tell him about Harry because I was afraid he would kill Harry, and go back to jail. I had absolutely no doubts that Harry would do the terrible things to me and my family that he threatened if I ever blabbed.

During the next three plus years Mom often took me to Harry's and Amy's. Sometimes she would get her hair done by Amy, take off, and leave me there while she ran errands or whatever.

Harry's idea of baby-sitting was that I was his "sex slave."

He told me many things over and over.

"You are nothing without me. You will lose your mind without my sex, because you will never have an orgasm with anyone but me. I own you." (*I did not have an orgasm until I married my second husband, Allan.*)

"You're candy money will stop."

"You are a murderer and God will never forgive you. You are condemned to live a life of hell."

"You owe the world a living; it's your job to sexually entertain me until death do us part."

Harry constantly messed with my mind. He rambled on about lots of religious mumbo-jumbo, confusing me about God, convincing me to be afraid of God who would strike me dead for all the evil inside me if I didn't perform sex stuff with Harry.

"God makes evil people like you to do evil things," Harry said, "and you make me do evil stuff. Your spirit is so unclean that only the fires of hell can purify it. And don't you EVER forget that if you ever tell, I will boil your body in oil, crush your bones with a sledge hammer, pulverize you and feed you to the dog so you will turn into shit and the maggots will eat you."

Even as a child, I wondered if someone didn't' tell Harry the same things he was telling me or was it the devil speaking through Harry's mouth?

One of Harry's recurring themes was that "Men have money, muscles, a dick, and balls and God gave us women to screw because they can't do anything else worthwhile."

Harry told me "X marks the spot. It's the blood of Satan. Z is on your forehead for Zeister. X is on your boobs, belly and your puss cause they all belong to Satan. You will be with the devil forever 'cause all women belong to the devil; there is no God."

He went on and on. "You need me to probe your butt hole or you will never shit again. The reason your daddy loves you is because he loves the smell of shit."

"God plays with people like puppets and cuts your strings when he's tired of you. You were born to suffer. You're scum and God walks on scum and doesn't care to hear your prayers so that is why he didn't stop me or save you. You will never be saved. There is no heaven, no Jesus; it's all a lie. I have planted seeds in you and you will grow more evil every day. Once others see your dark-stained spirit, they won't want to have anything to do with you anymore. God is a schizophrenic who called himself Jesus and the prince of darkness. And you're a miserable bitch just like your mother; a dirty rotten slut, rotten to the core and nothing can save your soul now."

The potential irony of it all recently hit me like a ton of bricks. In reflecting back, I probably would have soon relegated the event - catching Mom and Harry in the bedroom - to a distant memory. They probably could have gotten away with it without getting in a dither that I would spill the beans. But, on the other hand, I might have blabbed at a future time when something might have sparked a memory. I really don't know. As my mother used to say, "Little pictures have big ears and a big mouth."

Part 2 - The Perpetrators

Taffy Pull

As I stated at the beginning of Chapter One, The Set-up, Mom and Dad both sexually abused me before Harry, the master torturer, brutalized and claimed me as his sex slave. What changed after Harry was that for several years I was now the sex object for three people instead of two.

It was like a taffy pull – me being the taffy – and Mom, Dad, and Harry tugging from three different directions. I felt like I was an outlet for their problems that somehow I must be causing.

My greatest need was for genuine, non-sexual, non-abusive love. That need never came close to being met. Harry didn't know how. And my parents didn't either.

Mom had two sisters who both died, leaving her an only child while a teen-ager. She married her first husband, Mr. Smith when she was about eighteen. They had two girls, Mary and Tish. Soon after Tish was born, Mom's mother died in a car crash. Mom blamed her father, who was driving drunk and survived the accident.

Mr. Smith died a few years later from colon cancer, leaving Mom a widow at age twenty-eight. Losing her sisters, mother and husband – especially her mother – left Mom very bitter toward God. She quit attending Catholic Mass, and did not allow the name Jesus to be spoken, or any praying or Bible reading in her house. Many years later, Mom's closest friend confided in me, confirming that Mom shared that her father was a perpetrator and had sexually abused Mom when she was a young girl.

My dad was born the last of thirteen children. He never married until age thirty-three when he married my mother. He was a rage-aholic and an alcoholic. Several years ago a nephew of his, Johnny, confirmed that the family had a history of incest. Dad's family was very dysfunctional, violent, and Dutch Reform, religious fanatics. He was considered the rebel of his family. Ironically, his nephew, Sparkie, said dad used to preach from a soap box as a nine-year-old boy. Of course, all the tendencies and potential of becoming any kind of minister had vanished by the time he married Mom. He was now Pentecostal, which conflicted with Mom being Catholic. Neither of them went to church -- with the exception of two times that Dad tried to get on the wagon and stop drinking. Lacking support of any kind, both efforts were brief.

Mom married Dad when Mary was nine, and Tish seven. Two more daughters resulted from this union: Doris Lee, 1942, and me, 1945 in Chicago, Illinois.

When I turned six months, my family moved from Chicago to a place they called the "Frog Farm" in upper New Jersey. It was a rat-infested, run-down old house located about a half-mile from the main road, and one hundred feet back from a lake that froze over every winter. A bridge just wide enough for one vehicle was our only route to the main road. One of the few joys of my young life was getting to ride in the rumble seat of Dad's Model A convertible. The wind would rustle my hair and I would feel so very much alive and free.

It was at the "Frog Farm" that my mother began to sexually abuse me. She rubbed Vicks all over my naked little body, filled my rectum with cold fluids, and manipulated my clitoris, sending me into convulsive states. As I grew, I remember her giving me regular enemas, forcing me to hold them until my belly knotted with pain. (*While attending a support group with me and my friend in the 70's, my sisters Mary and Doris Lee confessed, remembering mom giving them enemas for a long time.*)

There was a lot of verbal and emotional abuse which increased when Dad got home, usually drunk. (*More about the resulting violence in the next chapter.*)

When I was about four-and-a-half, Dad and Mother's dad built the house in Ramsey, New Jersey. Mom's dad gave my parents a lot of money toward building the house. It was built in an upper class neighborhood, across the street from the owner of the town newspaper.

Dad built the New England style home with a small front porch. It was a two story house; white with black shutters, a basement and an unfinished attic. After we lived there a couple years, they semi finished half of the attic into a bedroom for Doris Lee and me. That is when I remember my father starting to sexually abuse me by oral copulation and finger penetration. He also sexually abused my sister, Doris Lee, who shared a bedroom with me. They thought I was asleep, but I lay awake; and heard everything.

It was after the ordeal at Harry's that the taffy pull began. Relentless: a sharp tug here; a heavy-handed yank there.

Harry played me against both parents, telling me terrible things about them and how I was going to be just like them. He worked hard to convince me that Mom and Dad were evil and so was I.

Mom played me against Dad and Tish, a diversion, to confuse my dad. But when things got too hot and heavy about Tish or money, Mom would start in on stuff about HIS daughters *(Doris Lee and I)*, their problems, and how she should never have married him. One on one, Mom concentrated on convincing me I was evil, that "God is punishing you for being born". She said I was a curse in her life.

Daddy kept me to himself, in that he didn't play me against anyone. From about two-and-a-half, he would sit me on his knee and tell me his woes, saying I was the only one who cared. *(This was way too much information for a kid to be told or to understand.)* I was his sanctuary, lover, and wife replacement. Daddy wasn't really there, like his body was; he always seemed a million miles away, lost somewhere in his thoughts. Whatever I was feeling or going through was oblivious to him. I was like a warm blankie to him.

My recollections during those years of Dad and Mom are powerful. The most striking difference between them was their eyes. Dad's eyes were of such a clear, sky blue that I felt I could look into them and see forever. I recall times that I sat on his knee and, while peering into his eyes, wondered what was back there. Mom's eyes had kind of a hazel tint but there was nothing pleasant about them. It was like looking into the eyes of a great white shark; scary without showing any light or reflection of life. Mom also had an opposite build than Dad.

She was built like a 200-plus pound fireplug, well, actually more like a barrel. She was about five-feet-five. Mom snored and Dad didn't. Both had false teeth except Mom only had an upper plate which shot out of her mouth sometimes when she would laugh. Laughing was merely a screen that Mom tried to hide behind. In reality, there was nothing funny in her life.

Mom knew about me and Dad. She came down to the basement one day and caught Dad perpetrating me. I was on top of the freezer, gyrating while Dad fingered me and rubbed my clitoris. Mom immediately said I was a dirty little girl as she turned and went back up stairs. She didn't say a word to my dad, who laughed and told me to put my panties back on and go out and play.

Of course, Mom knew about me and Harry. But I don't believe that Harry knew about me and Dad or me and Mom, unless Mom told him during their intimate times.

Dad knew about me and Mom. He did catch on; I'm sure, about me and Harry, when the latter, in a drunken boast, said "I screwed your wife and baby girl." A fight ensured, blood flowed, police came, and there was more jail time for Dad. He got blamed for starting the fight, because Mom and Harry told their story and a little girl's story didn't count.

Sex at Five-and-a-Half

Vengeful eyes behind the physical thrust,
all driven by a demon called lust.

Ecstasy that seems like pleasure,
while I must remain calm.

Things begin to intensify, then joy explodes from inside.

Was I pleasing, or was it pleasure?

I'm relaxed now, or did I die?

I don't understand!

Daddy Is That You?

Joy, comfort, a tender touch, safety, and knowing who to trust.
Daddy, is that you?

Kind expressions, feeling reassured, believing in every word.
Emotions begin to rise, from deep inside.
Daddy, is that you?

Strange lustful eyes, a familiar smell, associated with pleasure.
Daddy, is that you?

All at once, passion, fear, shame, blame, exploding in every direction.
Daddy, is that you?

Confused, embarrassed, feeling dirty, mutilated, and empty.
Daddy, is that you?

War Zone

The title for this chapter is exactly what our home was at times, with the seeds of violence pouring out of a bottle into my father. Dad drank whiskey, ale and mom's cooking sherry if nothing else was around. He would come home at least two sheets in the wind, get drunker during the evening then drink all week-end. The booze fueled his anger.

A variety of things triggered his explosions. Money was discussed a lot; the lack of it and how much Tish got. It could be dirty dishes, not enough food in the refrigerator, old food in the refrigerator, Mom's refusal to buy more beer, Tish getting her own phone line and phone. A constant biggie was Mom's hygiene, or rather, extreme lack of hygiene. To my best recollection, she never bathed more than three or four times a year: Easter, mid-summer, Thanksgiving, and Christmas.

Dad's rages sometimes elevated from yelling in a gruff voice to punching Mom out cold with his fist. When Daddy pushed Mom down the cellar stairs in the Ramsey house, I got in his face screaming, "I hate you! I hate you! I hate you!" He shoved me away. I got right back in his face and repeated, still screaming, "I hate you! I hate you! I hate you!" He forcefully squeezed my arms, picked me up by the arms and set me back about four feet. He glared into my eyes, and with great anger, said "Stay away from me and stay out of this."

My sense of fear took over. I knew at that moment I could be next down the stairs. I shut up. Doris Lee called the doctor.

The tumble down the stairs broke both of Mom's ankles. Dad grabbed another beer and sat silent at the kitchen table. Mom told the doctor she slipped and fell down the stairs.

Dad repeatedly pulled the phone lines out of the wall, killed the pet chickens, shot the cats, and drowned our kittens. During one frightening rage he took an axe to the living room furniture, baby grand piano, then cut the couch open with his pocket knife and pulled the stuffing out. He smashed a three-foot diameter gold-glass fish bowl *(which mom said came from Germany)* into smithereens and ground it into the hard wood floor with the hammer side of the axe.

Many nights Mom, Doris Lee, and I would wait in our car, up the road, for the lights in our house to go out before we would go home. Our favorite spot to park was in McClellan's driveway. We would get a clear view through the trees behind the houses and see when dad would turn the lights off. I went to school tired a lot.

The hygiene factor provided rage fodder for years. Dad burned several pairs of Mom's shoes, dresses, and bras. To my knowledge, Mom didn't wear underwear. She exposed herself at times when gardening or cleaning. I had my "picture taken" by her "brownie" as she sat in a chair with her dress up above her knees. Just now while writing this, the thought occurred to me that this is the reason why I don't like to wear dresses. Come to think of it, none of my sisters like to wear dresses either. Mary is known to wear skirts or dresses when she attends dog shows. She's now in her 70's.

The more I think about it, I always wondered why any man would want to get intimate with Mom, because of the smell. Mr. Houston *(the black man she had an on-going affair with)*, Harry, and my dad either all had a poor sense of smell, or they got turned on by stench. Mom's pheromones mixed with body odor and her cheap perfume made for a bad mix.

An irony in the whole situation was that Dad's occupation was cesspool cleaner. He pumped out cesspools for a living and the kids at school knew it. Everyone knew everyone in Ramsey. So I guess it was natural for some of the kids to nickname me "Zesspool."

I confess that the nickname covered more ground than just Dad's vocation. Mom's poor hygiene translated into her kids having poor hygiene. My teeth had a green coating most of my childhood years due to lack of care. Mom never trained us to brush. It was during my sixteenth year before I had my teeth cleaned and began brushing on a regular basis. I am lucky to have most of my natural teeth.

What Makes You Want To Do That?

What makes you want to do that?
("It's because I love you.")
People don't hurt people they love, do they?

What makes you want to do that?
("It's because you're pretty and you smell so good.")
That doesn't give you the right, does it?

What makes you want to do that?
("It feels so good!")
Not to me, it doesn't, does it?

What makes you want to do that to "ME"?
("You're special, my favorite, and I know you won't tell,
will you?!")
Deafening rage blocks out what I want to yell.
Every time you do that.

Sisterly Love, Say What?

At our house, being the youngest of four girls had serious disadvantages. Mary was thirteen years older than me, Tish eleven years, and Doris Lee four years.

Mary was the same height as Mom, about five foot five, although shapely rather than fat. She was always tinting her hair because it turned white at a very young age. She had this very annoying habit of sucking air through her lips and snorting like a pig. Mary was mostly indifferent to what was happening. She spent a lot of time and energy avoiding physical confrontations with my Dad who was step-dad to her and Tish. She said I was daddy's little brat.

I felt a lot of resentment from Mary and very little love. She did most of the house work and babysitting. She was really kind of, not there, if you know what I mean. Over the years, she remained indifferent, distant, and would angrily tell me I was just like my father. I never figured out what she was referring to, nor did I ask, because she would never discuss anything, very much like mom. There was definitely a communication problem at our house.

Tish was the tallest of us four girls; about five-feet-nine, big-boned but neither fat nor skinny. She had a white streak in her hair as a mid-teen-ager. I always looked at it as her being a skunk with that streak. She convinced me that I was not a nice person. Tish had this habit of sitting and chewing on the cuticles on her fingers and toes; she filed her finger nails relentlessly. Tish never tried to disguise her dislike of me, an unwanted half-sister. She was insecure, hateful, mean, selfish, greedy, and spiteful. I was like an integral part of a game she loved to play. I'd call it saboteur trains scapegoat. She would do things to get me into trouble and then "punish" me for it. When she babysat me, she hit me on the head, face, butt, legs, and arms. She locked me in a closet for hours until I cried myself to sleep. She would also tie a rope around my chest, lower me into the outhouse at the "Frog Farm," and let me hang there amongst the flies, maggots, roaches, and stench for what seemed like forever.

Tish's usual lecture was like a broken record. "I'm the boss. You better not forget it. Do not squeal to Mommy or Daddy or I will drop you in and not pull you out . . . EVER!" Her mouth was tight. Her eyes squeezed almost closed as she sneered into my eyes with hate.

I remember her locking me in the cellar with spiders, rats, worms, and other creepy, crawly creatures. It was cold, damp, and scary. I cried a lot when Tish babysat me.

She was good at brain washing. "The truth is what I say. What everybody else says is LIES . . . ALL LIES. God does not love you . . . because you are stupid, ugly, and a liar." I felt so alone, unloved and unwanted.

Variously, Tish choked my neck with her hands, her scarves, and one of her belts. The belt left a mark and scared her. Afraid someone would ask what happened, she didn't use a belt to choke me anymore.

Dad paid for Mary and Tish to go to college; they became grade school teachers and each taught for over twenty years.

Dad entrusted Mom with the profits from the sale of the house in Jersey for our college funds. Mom gave the money to Trish to buy her own house. Doris Lee and I never saw a nickel of that money to go to college.

Over the years, Tish treated me like I was the chamber maid. I was allowed to clean her room and, later, to come to her house to clean and do her laundry, baby-sit her daughter, and prepare dinner for her truck driver husband. I felt from an early age that she hated my guts. I'm sure she still does; but to this day, I do not understand WHY!

Doris Lee and I were a lot closer, until I was about five-and-a-half. After that, we fought like cats and dogs. Again, I don't know why. She had previously been a comfort to me. She saw me and Dad, because she was in the other twin bed in the room we shared. He would go from her bed to mine, and vice-versa. She would often wait for him to leave, then come into my bed and we would comfort one another, mostly me because I cried a lot. Doris Lee also knew about my mother as she told me, Mom did the same stuff to her (*enemas*) until she started menstruation.

Before Doris Lee reached age ten she turned on me with consistency. She tried to smother me with a pillow – two or three times. Once when Mom was at the neighbor's, she nailed me inside a cut-out cubby hole behind the drywall in the attic. I could barely move; the heat began to suffocate me, panic set in, and only very intense screaming got Doris Lee to let me out. Another time she tied me up with clothes line and laid a six-foot, dead-stinking-rotten black snake on me – "So," as Doris Lee explained, "the stink will become part of your skin and you will smell like Mommy."

She took a peeling knife from the kitchen and carved out several gum-looking shapes from a bar of Ivory soap. I was none the wiser when she extended a Chicklets gum box and offered me a piece. She laughed long and hard as I gagged and begged for help in getting it out of my mouth and off my teeth. I got a bad dose of diarrhea.

As a teen-ager, Doris Lee eventually ran away from home, only to come back. Then Dad went into a rage one day when she was in the bathroom (*not to be confused with the outhouse which was at the "Frog Farm"*). He got his own blood everywhere as he punched his fists through the locked door. Doris escaped through the bathroom window and ran away again. She later returned, but kept her distance from me.

In high school, Doris Lee was an upperclassman while I was a freshman. We were sometimes mistaken for each other. But never again after an episode happened which changed Doris Lees' appearance. She had a wake-up-in-the-middle-of-the-night experience with what she believed to be some sort of vile, demonic entity that terrified her. She had such a fright that her eyes had the appearance of having just been surprised by a flash bulb. Following this episode, her thyroid became over-active causing her eyes to have a beady look that lasted for years.

It was when I was about nine and Doris Lee thirteen that Harry finally got the leper treatment. No more trips to his house. We weren't allowed to talk about him. One more fight between him and Dad and there might have been a dead body.

Incest, My Dependent Alliance

Was I Daddy's precious little princess, or his love goddess?
Did I innocently seek reassurance,
or sinfully clutch onto carnality?

Daddy's addiction empowered him with control
to maneuver me through shame, forging my mind like steel,
to focus on his impure sinful acts,
which pillaged me of my chastity.

Coerced and confused, my love-torn heart concealed the truth.
Kept it near and dear, like a fragile bird,
careful not to expose it to the elements.
Per chance I might die.

This secret, like a vampire's bite, made me his possession.
A temptress. lurking by night, dependent on him to survive.
A zombie by day, I continued to pray.
Yet death came not to a ghoul; such as I.

The Priest

During the years as sex object of Dad and Harry, I broke silence to three people outside our family.

I confided in the grade school nurse, and one of the teachers. My grade school was red brick with two upper floors and a basement. The nurse's station was on the first floor close to the main office. It was the nurse who had become aware of my many physical problems and heard my complaints. I regularly complained of ear aches, headaches, belly aches, stomach aches and a loud noise inside my head. I trusted her. She summoned my mother which upset me. I panicked; begged her not to call my mommy and began crying. The nurse reassured me everything would be fine. When Mom arrived, the nurse shared some of what I had told her. She asked Mom if she was aware of any of this, and if there could be any problems at home.

Very bluntly, Mom said, "Barbara Jean watches too much TV and has an over-active imagination. She will do anything to get out of class or to get attention."

The matter was dropped; at least as far as the school was concerned. From that point on, whenever I went to the nurse she would just let me lie on the cot and comfort me from time to time. She didn't call my mom again. But it certainly wasn't a dead issue with Mom. She nailed me with that look, leaned close to my face, and warned, "I will take you back to see Harry for another week if you talk to anybody. STOP TELLING SUCH LIES!" I was so confused.

Mom did have a way of getting my undivided attention. I was almost afraid to even say "Hi" to anybody for a while, becoming introverted with a very low self esteem. I eventually shared with a girl who lived at the end of our street that I was having sex with my dad. She said she was having sex with her step-dad. I used to visit with her sometimes at her house. But not again after the time her dad forced me to watch him sexually abuse her.

Doris Lee knew about what had happened. She told me, "Drop the whole thing; forget it ever happened or you could die. Do you wanna die?"

With all that was going on with me incestuously, I began to stop in at the cobble stone church on the corner of Cherry and Darlington. I was in the second grade. I would light a candle for all those who were evil, including me. "Dear God," I would ask, "please take the bad things out of my head and take the hell from our home and hearts. Please love me again and clean my black soul."

One day the priest came out and looked at me. "Why are you lighting so many candles? They are not toys, you know."

I looked up at him; he was stocky like Friar Tuck. "The devil is in my heart and hurting everyone in my family and I need God to answer my prayers to save me."

The priest reached out, took my small hand in his and led me into the back room where he kept his robes. I told him about some of the evils. He let go of my hand, turned to face me and exposed his erection. Listening to my concerns he became aroused, "This is the devil's tail," he said. "Choke it real hard and you will get rid of the evil."

My heart was pounding and I was afraid he would hurt me if I didn't do what he told me to. After he came, he rubbed "the devil's vomit" all over my face. He re-fastened his robe and tried to teach me some Catholic prayers. I was numb and did some mumbling, then left in a daze.

Now I couldn't even go back to the church to talk to God. Instead, I started to go to the brook in the woods behind our house to talk to God there. I would find garden snakes and frogs and talk to them. I knew they wouldn't tell on me.

Silently In the Dark

*Waiting in her twilight state, unexpectedly she was alerted by his
lascivious manipulative touch, silently in the dark.*

*Quiet as a church mouse, she endured his carnal acts,
while observed by another,
silently in the dark.*

*Shame interacted with pleasure, pain wrenched at her emotions, which
she submitted with obedience,
silently in the dark.*

*She felt like a nasty exhibition, ruptured into
sharp-edged pieces that severed her love,
silently in the dark.*

*Mortified, shrouded with guilt,
nausea and confusion submerged her,
silently in the dark.*

*In an ocean of tears, once again, she lay lamenting,
silently in the dark.*

Bye-bye, New Jersey

It was when I was thirteen, after I announced that my menstruation cycle had begun, that Dad stopped having sex with me.

As previously stated, Mom stopped her abuse of me at about the same time. No more enemas. No more physical contact; not ever a hug. But Mom continued to hold a power over me. Like I had to do whatever she said or she would reject me, and I would have no mother. I developed a strong fear of rejection that would later bind me for years in an unholy marriage to my first husband, Jack.

My older sisters, Mary and Tish, had secured husbands and meal tickets away from home. Then it was Doris Lee's turn. Ward was her fiancé. But that didn't stop him from raping me when I was about thirteen-and-a-half. I was spending the night at his parents' house as his sister Lory's guest. Ward was a six foot, medium built Italian guy with olive skin and black hair. He looked somewhat like Eddie Fisher, but not as much as his brother Ned did. Ned was much better looking. While I was in the shower, my hair full of shampoo, Ward stepped in, grabbed me from behind and rammed me several times. "Tight bitch!" he said while still cupping my breasts with his hands. I grabbed his hands which he jerked out of my soapy grasp. He shoved me away and said, "Wash up, you filthy slut." I recognized his voice; felt his class ring and knew it was Ward.

While drying myself, crying I cautiously left the bathroom and dashed to Lory's bedroom. Her response to what I told her was not what I expected. She looked scared as she said, "He thought it was me. Don't tell anyone. It will get me in trouble. Ward will beat the crap out of me. Dad will choke me to death. Forget it ever happened."

I was scared to sleep there; and did so only because Lory assured me it never happens in the bedroom, only in the bathroom.

When I told Doris Lee, she did not want to hear about it. She snapped, "You're making that up to get attention!" She pulled away from me after that and the distance never again really closed. It seemed that it would years later, but it turned out to be only a temporary hope.

Mom decided to leave dad because he wouldn't change his ways; stop drinking and raging and beating her up. Mom, Doris Lee and I moved in with Bart and Mary for a while.

Bart complicated his alcoholism by being a rage-a-holic. Bart was over six feet tall, black hair and looked a lot like Dean Martin. He served in the armed forces where he learned strict discipline which he applied to his parenting tactics.

While staying at Bart and Mary's, Bart decided to teach me a lesson. To teach me "not to whine and be a tattle-tale to your mommy" he picked me up by my left arm and left leg and threw me against the wall, grinning while I plopped down from the wall onto my twin bed. I had a real bad headache for the rest of the day and cried for a long time. Bart always called me a spoiled brat and a cry baby. All I wanted was a hug and some kind words.

To teach their family dog not to chew things Bart tied a shoe in Ginger's mouth with a belt and left it there for days and repeatedly beat her.

To teach one of his sons not to rock, he destroyed the rocking chair in the house and wouldn't let any more in. This didn't stop Willy from rocking. He managed to rock in any chair he sat in. It was Willy's way of coping. Willy still rocks to this day.

And to teach his other son, Ben not to lose his 39-cent thong slippers, Bart beat him with a wide belt, leaving welts from the base of his neck to the back of his heels; the welts turned black and blue.

When Willy and Ben were two and four, they were so cute the local photography studio placed their pictures in the lighted display in front of the Studio.

When Ben was an adult he tried to talk truth about his abusive past with his mother who refused to discuss it. I encouraged her to talk it out with Ben so he could begin to heal old wounds. Mary didn't speak to me for over fifteen years, until the day of Ben's funeral. The talk was short and superficial.

Dad convinced Mom that he had changed so she, Doris Lee, and I moved back in with him. He did go back on the wagon and even attended church; however, getting no support from Mom, and her not changing her ways or her hygiene habits –

"You no good Catholic bitch!" – He gave up church and turned back to the bottle. War zone again.

Mary, Bart, their two boys, Tish and her daughter, Liz, moved in 1958 to Arizona; all living in the same house. Mary and Tish took the Arizona certification exam and secured teaching positions in a west Phoenix school district.

It was about a year later, after my periods started and Mom and Dad separated, that Mom, Doris Lee, and I moved to Arizona. That was in 1959.

Again, we were all living with Mary and Bart's family. Mom's immediate motivation was getting as far away from Dad as possible as Tish was also desperate to get away from her ex-husband. Tish had met the guy while she was an airline flight attendant. He was Lebanese, about five foot ten inches tall, sort of stocky, black hair, olive complexion and well dressed. I am sure that Tish thought he had money. They got married and for Tish reality set in. Less than six months of ironing his underwear she had the marriage annulled.

When we moved to Arizona, I thought things would change to the better. But even with this move I could not get away from abuse.

We were in Phoenix about three months when Tish found a house she wanted to buy. She convinced Mom to give her the money that Dad had given to Mom with instructions that it be used for college educations for Doris Lee and me. The money went for the down payment. Mom, Doris Lee, and I moved in with Tish and her daughter Liz.

Shortly after moving into Tish's new house, a guy named Ted, who lived with his sister across the street, began flirting with me. He offered to take me for a ride in his red 1959 Chevy convertible. After he found out I was fifteen, he quickly turned his attention to Trish. Tish and Ted soon began an affair. Ted was recently divorced and had one son from that marriage. Trish and Ted, a truck driver, got married with Ted moving in with her. Ted was about six feet tall. He looked like he lifted weights. He wasn't very good looking in the face, but he had a GQ way about him that Trish was attracted to. Ted looked like a less handsome Steve McQueen.

I was fifteen, going to Carl Hayden High School, and looking for a way out; either a job for which I would be considered too young or a husband. Whichever came first; I was all for it.

There was a Bob's Big Boy in Phoenix at Central and Thomas that was popular among teen-agers. I was eating a hot fudge sundae with my girl friend Deedee, who had driven us there, when Jack zoned in on me. "You're gonna sure get fat," he smiled while nodding toward the sundae. "Give me your phone number. I'll call you about a date."

Jack swept in like the Court Jester, funny, with a mesmerizing way about him. I was in awe. He was six-feet-one, thin, with a jagged scar on his left cheek, the result of a car accident. He looked like he could be Tom Jones' brother.

That was in February, 1961. We were married on November 25 the same year. I was sixteen and five months. Jack was nineteen-and-a-half.

Most definitely I saw marriage as a way out of the house. What I didn't see was that I had jumped from the frying pan into the fire.

Jack went into the Air Force not long after we were married. He saw it as a way to get a free education. But his career as Uncle Sam's man in blue crash landed after little more than a year with him getting beaten black and blue after making a pass and trying to jump the bones of the wrong serviceman. His AC-DC tendencies made it difficult for him.

It was while Jack was still in the Air Force and I was living alone with my cats in a two bedroom apartment that Dad had moved from New Jersey. At Mom's insistence, he moved in with me. One morning when I woke up he was sitting on my bed staring at me. I told him to get out of my room and never come back in without my permission. That day I went out to buy a lock for my bedroom door. When I got back, Dad had moved out. He went to live with a brother in Riverside, California.

Meanwhile, with Jack still in the service, I went to stay with him at off-base housing in Texas and Georgia. Jack's dad, EC drove me down in a 1955 Buick he bought for Jack and me. When EC and I were spending the night at a hotel in New Mexico, EC tried to have sex with me. I will share more about that in the next chapter.

After Jack graduated from boot camp, he got stationed in Savanna Georgia. It was in Georgia that Jack and I conceived our first-born. Jack sent me back to Phoenix to live with Mom and take care of the necessary paperwork to secure for him a hard luck discharge from the Air Force and deliver our first child. The discharge went through while Jack was still in Georgia.

Jack got to come home to witness the birth of our daughter, Paula. He returned to Georgia to await his honorable discharge. Jack got out of the Air Force, moved back to Phoenix when Paula was three months old. He and I rented a three-bedroom house in Phoenix. Six months later we conceived our second child, Holly. I was delighted to be a mother again.

Remember my fear of rejection? Well, I believe that had a lot to do with my marriage to Jack lasting twelve years. He did many perverted things to me and molested our two daughters. He admitted to liking sex with both men and women. Jack brought women into the house and had sex with them in our bed. He did it even while I was in the hospital having our second child. The girl he was with that night told me about it a few years later. It made me sick thinking about it.

I didn't see Dad again until I was twenty-one and my second daughter was six weeks old. Mom and I took the bus to see Dad in Riverside as he was dying of cancer.

A short time later, unknowing to me, he moved in with my mother, at Tish's house, confined to a twin bed in Mom's room. No one let me know he was in town until I went over to visit Mom. Dad was upset that I hadn't come sooner. I felt guilty, even scared that he wouldn't love me anymore and die while thinking badly of me. I explained that no one had let me know he was there. He just took in my words without reacting.

I helped change his diapers, clean the poop from under his nails (*he would dig in his feces*), massage his calves and feet, shave him and comb his hair. He never brought up what he had done to me – and, respectfully, to please God and honor Mom and Dad – I did not say anything either.

Mom worked at Montgomery Ward's, Tish taught school, Ted drove a truck and I would stay with Dad until Mom got home. During one of the early visits, Dad asked me what I had done with all of the money he had been sending me for college; also, why hadn't I answered any of his letters. "What money? What letters?"

"I gave your mother money to send you and your sister Doris Lee to college…"

"I sent you $75 in a letter every month."

"You're lying. I never got any money or letters."

Dad proved his case by having his sister-in-law in Riverside send over the canceled checks so I would know that he was telling me the truth. I chewed Mom out; Dad chewed her out too. What had happened is that Mom would open all the envelopes, take out the money, and get rid of the envelopes and letters. Her defense; "It went for room and board; this way the money didn't get wildly spent." She had forged my signature on all the checks she had cashed. That went on for over three years without me ever being the wiser. What tiny amount of respect I might have had for Mom went up in smoke.

During Dad's final weeks, he never came close to saying he was sorry about anything, which is what I most wanted to hear. "Forgive him, for he knew not what he did," a voice inside my head kept repeating until he died. I said the Lord's Prayer as the morticians took his body away.

I did feel loved by Dad; that is, I felt that I had meant something to him. I felt frustrated and angry at the same time. Frustrated, because my dad and I never got to talk truth; angry he left me to live the lies with unloving, spiteful sisters and Mom.

Jack gave little to no support for my grief. He acted like I had not experienced a loss.

Jack told me during our love making how when he was about nine, he would do oral sex with his grandmother while she pretended to sleep. While still in grade school he paid his school buddies to "let him butt fuck them."

"Listen to me," Jack said, "you will do everything I tell you to do. The Bible says, "Wives, obey your husband's" and anything a husband and wife do is okay in the eyes of God." With Jack, "everything" included three-ways and yours truly having sex with one of his friends so he could watch me.

I cooked, ironed, and did laundry – free, of course – for his trucker friends.

Submitting to participation in vile, perverted, disgusting sex acts only seemed to fuel Jack's desire to have me be the focal point of his sexual experimentation. Once he used a Polaroid and took close-ups of my vaginal area. "I want to keep them to look at while I'm out of town on the road." Jack drove truck from Phoenix to Los Angeles and back. Years later – after marrying my second husband, Allan, I found one of those photos in his wallet. I asked him how he got it, because I knew that he used to drive a truck for the same company Jack had worked for. He said that Jack had sold several photos to his trucker buddies and had given one to him. I was so livid that I contacted Jack to let him have an earful. He laughed and said, "No one knew it was your pussy in the photos . . . until you told Allan. He didn't know either...DUMMY!"

My past swirled in my head; the constant brainwashing, the threats – and now realizing I was a high school drop-out on top of agreeing to "for better or worse". I did whatever he told me to do; with little hope of any kind of employment – and soon two young daughters. And no place to go but back home, I blocked out all thoughts of escape. I was actually afraid that Jack would leave me.

Following dad's death and finding out about Jack's affair with Judy, I suffered an anxiety attach and tried to commit suicide. I was admitted to a mental ward at a private institution off Camelback Road. I had slit my right forearm. The psychiatrist who interviewed me told me I was a danger to myself and my children which snapped me back into reality and the desire to LIVE so I wouldn't lose my children. I was released about three weeks later.

When our daughters were 4 and 2, I turned to my faith in God and believed our daughters and I would make it somehow without Jack. I filed for divorce. Neither of us contested it so we were divorced within a few months. Jack moved out as soon as I filed for the divorce to live with two guys in an apartment across town.

Unable to find work and wanting to get as far away from Jack as I could, I bravely put everything I could carry, along with our daughters into my 1963 oxidized red Volkswagen Bug; drove to Hollywood, California and started a new life. Not knowing if I would find a job or a place to live, I was scared. First thing I did when we got to Hollywood, was find a room at a hotel.

While living in the hotel, I met George who rented a room down the hall. This was before he became a famous comedian. He and I would sit on the balcony after my girls were asleep; drink a totty and talk about all sorts of things. George and I never dated, we were just friends. George did take me to see Janis Joplin at the Hollywood Bowl, which I will forever remember as a great time.

The girls and I ate a lot of peanut butter sandwiches during the time I diligently searched the paper for a job. On my first interview at Brant Wallpaper Company, I was hired as the front desk receptionist/secretary. I praised God for showing me the way to gainful employment.

After my second paycheck, I decided the girls and I needed to find an apartment, which proved to be a challenge. Everywhere I went no one allow kids, but did take animals. I thought that odd and cruel. I finally found a two bedroom apartment just up the hill from Capitol Records, off Hollywood and Vine. Michael Cole and his wife lived in the apartment cross the way. Michael Cole was one of the male stars on the TV show, Mod Squad. They were very nice and welcomed us with fresh brownies and milk.

Michael's wife told me about a lady who worked for the State; said the lady would find a place for my daughters in a pre-school run by the state and it wouldn't cost me any money. After meeting me and my girls, this angel of a woman over road a one year waiting list so my girls could attend school while I worked.

Michael's wife babysat for me when I went on a date. I dated two men during my stay in California. The first fellow, Leo, was a momma's boy and possessive. I quickly ended that relationship. Bill was a postman. He and I dated several months. He took the girls and me to movies, the zoo, Griffith Park on picnics and always stopped at the Dairy Queen before returning us to our apartment.

Jack kept calling me every day at work; would talk to me for over an hour each time. He would wait on hold while I answered calls that came in. He spoke honey soaked words of love to me, telling me he'd changed his ways; quit drinking, stopped womanizing and wanted to be a "FAMILY" again. He finally talked me into letting him fly out to see us and talk to me about getting re-married.

When we met Jack at the airport, the girls were very excited to see their daddy. I was moved by this and wanted a "family' for their sake, hoping Jack had indeed changed, but not trusting that he had. First thing I noticed was his hair. Jack always had very curly hair and wore it like an afro, sometimes short, sometimes long. He had straightened his hair, thinking it made him look handsome. I told him it was "different", adding it looked fake and plastered to his head and I didn't like it as much as when it's natural.

Jack spent the night, but he wasn't allowed to touch me. Still being afraid of rejection, I listened to his words that I now look back on as "baffling me with bullshit". His words were what I wanted to hear to convince myself he had indeed changed. The girls and I lived in Holllywood for about a year before returning to Arizona about a month after Jack's visit.

Jack's mom and dad babysat the girls while he and I road with Jack's friend and his wife to Yuma to get re-married. During the ceremony I could feel Jack wasn't really into it. Jack's friend's wife told me later, she didn't think he was sincere, but could see commitment written all over my face as I said my vows.

That night, we stayed at a hotel in Yuma. I was hoping for a second honeymoon with adoring romance. Jack said he was tired and had a headache.

On the trip back to Phoenix, Jack pulled into a quick stop store to buy something. When he came out with a six pack of Coors, I immediately questioned his drinking and going back on his word. He told me, "Shut up Bitch, I run this marriage". I knew I had made a mistake right then and there. Rejection clothed my emotions as I felt imprisoned once again.

Meanwhile, my existence was one of feeling dirty, sinful, shameful, and hopelessly trapped in a situation to which I saw no EXIT sign.

Jack was sneaky, a liar and a cheat. The more subtle the perpetrator, the more difficult it is to address. Jack was very subtle, but in the end, I caught him molesting both our girls. He was back to his old ways and showed no love in his heart for me or our children.

It wasn't until our twelfth and last year of marriage that I would seek counseling through the state hospital, get my GED, find a job, and file for our second divorce. Paula was nine, Holly seven.

Little Miss Desperado

Little Miss Desperado was new and unknowing.
It all seemed like such a natural part of growing.

Curious to learn and so full of joy,
she was easily pleased by a simple little toy.

She strolled in the sun, down her bright sunny path.
At that time she feared nothing except for God's wrath!

As she walked down her path one bright sunny morning,
she was suddenly snatched up without any warning.

She was conditioned by force with coercion and threats.
At times it was like she was part of their bets.

Watching those treacherous thieves, ruthless thug and
slimy vipers, she soon came to realize they were
really nothing like her.

She was never allowed to ask the question why,
just to do what she's told, shut up or die.

She was taught to fear everything that came near,
and never allowed to shed a tear.

Conned by these deceivers, she lost sight of her way,
on that bright sunny path, on that bright sunny day.

She was lied to and tricked with incestual vicious pranks,
never even given so much as a thanks.

They near killed herself love,
insisted she completely depend on them,
which diligently kept her wondering,
who, what, why, where, and when.

They also kept her busy, feeling crazy and dizzy,
far away from the how,
leaving her no time to seek out the how,
oh dear God, what will she ever do now?

All through her pain, God kept sight of her inside desire,
as He kindled and fanned that tiny little fire.

When God saw that she could not bear any more,
He empowered her with hope, and a key to the door.

No longer a prisoner, set free by God's wrath,
Little Miss Desperado is back on her bright sunny path.

Predators

Although the advent of my menstruation did stop sexual abuse from Dad and Mom, I did not know how to stop the never-ending treadmill of abuse by others.

Therapists would later tell me that perpetrators recognize victims, spotting them in a crowd by the way they walk and act, then target those victims like a jungle predator does its prey.

Whatever the tell-tale signs were that cloaked me; I was spotted often over three decades. Even as a child I asked myself and God, "What can I do to stop this? Should I be stinker like Mom? What did I do to deserve this?"

As I grew from childhood into married adulthood, I felt doomed to the lifestyle that seemed to be some sort of private prison prepared for me. I knew what I was doing was wrong, yet I didn't believe I could break the cycle. Eventually, the fear of physical manhandling drove me to take self-defense classes and to read self-help books such as CO-DEPENDENCY, THE ART OF SELFISHNESS, and DANCING WITH ANGER.

There were predators all around me.

With my first father-in-law, the molestation was verbal. I was sixteen, and we were on our way to Wichita Falls, Texas, driving our '55 Buick, to join Jack, who had just graduated from boot camp. At a motel in New Mexico, E.C. said, "I want to prepare you for sex with Jack, teach you what to expect. We'll do it orally so you won't have to worry about getting pregnant. We won't have intercourse."

I could feel my face turning red. I grabbed my cat, which was in his cage, pillow, jacket, suitcase, and left the room to begin the walk back to Phoenix.

E.C. followed me in the car, begging me to get in, while I yelled at him, "You're a sick, evil man! You're never going to touch me in that way, EVER!"

He swore he wouldn't do anything, promised nothing would happen, and said, "I was wrong; I am sorry; please don't tell my wife."

I went back to the motel. E.C. got on his knees and asked God to forgive him; he again told me he was sorry and that it would never happen again. I didn't sleep all night.

After his dad got on the plane in Wichita Falls, I told Jack what had happened. He laughed. "Dad was just trying to help our sex life. Forget it ever happened. Don't tell Mom."

Upon Jack's return to civilian life, he drove a truck for the man who would years later become my second father-in-law. The semi-trucks were parked in the large area behind Pete's house. I suspected that Jack was cheating on me, having sex with a girl in one of the trucks. Pete was drunk as he walked me out to the yard. On the way to turn on the flood lights, we had to pass between a truck cab and a trailer parked close together. He led the way. Half-way, he turned around, grabbed both my breasts and said, "You sure do have nice titties!" I slapped him. He laughed, then turned around and flipped on the lights and went back to the house.

Later when I told Jack what had happened, he said, "Forget it ever happened or you'll get me fired."

My sister Tish's husband Ted was a predator. During the time I was living with Mom in Tish's house while Jack was in Georgia in the Air Force, Ted preyed on me. I was eight months pregnant and had returned to Phoenix to have the baby. Coming back one day from visiting a friend, I entered the living room. Ted and his buddy John were there, both drunk. John grabbed me; both fondled my breasts and mauled me with their hands. John grabbed my butt and said, "Come on, baby. One of us wants to fuck you while you suck the other's dick."

I fought my way loose and left the house. I was afraid to go in the house after that without someone else being there other than Ted or his buddy. I didn't tell anyone right away, but eventually told Jack when he came home on leave for the baby's birth. Three guesses what he said. You got it: "Forget it ever happened. All you will do is start trouble."

Jack's friends Dutch, Tom, and Dudley were predators.

Just past eight months pregnant and Jack still in Georgia, Dutch asked if I'd go with him to get a burger and a hot fudge sundae at Bob's Big Boy at 19th Avenue and Bethany Home Road. I thought it would be nice. As we were finishing off the burgers, Dutch said, "I sure would like to fuck you." He said it loud enough for others to hear. "You're a pig!" I said. I got up and went outside to begin the five-mile walk to Tish's house.

Dutch came after me, grabbed me, and tried to kiss me. "I can't get you pregnant because you already are. So what's the problem?"

He finally convinced me to get into his car and he took me home without saying another word. I didn't see him again until nearly three decades later at a car reunion. I had my daughter, Paula, with me; walked up to him and, in front of his friends, introduced him to Paula. "This is the child I was nearly nine months pregnant with twenty-seven years ago when you asked to fuck me."

Dutch turned red-faced and said, "You hit below the belt." I said, "I've waited a long time to get even by embarrassing you like you did me."

Tom made his move while Jack was on the truck driving cattle to California. He came to the door and asked to borrow Jack's spare hot shot (*electric cattle prod*). When I went to get it, Tom let himself in the house, just walked in, uninvited. He approached me in the kitchen. "I want to eat you out and fuck your brains out." Incensed, I grabbed my cast-iron frying pan, hit him on the head twice, and said, "Get the hell out of my house!"

Knocked goofy, Tom laughed and said, "You'd probably be a lousy fuck anyway."

It was during a short separation from Jack that Dudley did his deed. I was renting an apartment and living there with my two daughters. I met Dudley at the sprint car races at Manzanita Speedway and he invited himself to a dinner date at my apartment.

Planning for a special evening, I had my neighbor watch my girls. I fixed a lovely dinner and awaited Dudley's arrival. He was on time and seemed nice enough, communicated well, complimented me on my clean apartment, good-smelling dinner, and remarked that I looked beautiful.

Right after dinner Dudley came on to me hot and heavy. "Slow down," I said. "I don't move that fast on a first date."

"You bitch!" he said. He slapped me, ripped my blouse off; tore my slacks off, then my bra and panties. He dragged me to my daughter's room, forcing me onto one of the beds. He forced me to swallow his erect penis, nearly smothering me. Something snapped in my head. In a panic for air, with millions of emotions flashing in my mind, I had to do something. With his penis down my throat as far as he could ram it and his hand holding my head with a fistful of hair, I bit down as hard as I could, making a side-to-side grinding motion as fast as I could, like a Gila monster.

It all happened so fast. He back handed me across the jaw, bouncing me against the wall. He grabbed my hair again and slammed me into the wall. "You fucking cunt! No good fucking bitch! Dirty slut!" He tucked his bleeding penis into his shorts, pulled up his Levi's and left in a hurry. I was relieved he didn't kill me.

In 1972, while working for an exterminating company, a job I'd had for only three months, the CEO asked me to stay late one Friday to take shorthand on a last-minute letter. Everybody else was gone when I entered his office, pad and pen in hand, and sat down in the chair facing his desk. He entered the room after me. I heard him lock the door and saw him come straight to me. He began to fondle me as I struggled. He was only five-foot-three but a mighty mouse-type guy. I got up and tried to get away. He tackled me and we fell to the floor with him on top. I kneed him in the groin, elbowed his nose, and broke his glasses. Blood spurted from his nose as he quickly withdrew into a fetal position. I got the door unlocked, grabbed my purse and keys, ran to my car, got in and locked the door while starting the engine. It was probably the fastest I ever got home. My career in the exterminating business was over.

Another boss did a number on me. I was a flight attendant for a charter airline. On one of our flights we stayed over in Orange County, California. The pilot was my supervisor. He knocked on my motel door, barged in, raped me then called me a slut. "Keep your mouth shut or we will all lose our jobs."

I quit flying.

There also were predator co-workers; even a seventy-year-old neighbor who tried to get physical. As I mentioned early in this book, it would take nearly five years of counseling and therapy for me to recover from all the victimizing done to me.

This Sticky Thing Called Pain

Like monkey snot, gluey pizza cheese,
this thing called pain holds on.

Stuck to it, co-dependently adhered,
resembling Siamese twins.

Fearful any attempt to separate would leave me alone,
with only death to face.

Decisions once denied me now so piercingly thrust my way,
terrified I'll cut my own throat.

Frustrated, anxiously seeking solutions to dissolve
the slime mucus.

This sticky thing called pain.

Nightmares

Eight separate terrifying dreams took turns playing in my mind over and over. For forty-plus years I endured the anguish of these recurring nightmares. There were times when I dreaded going to sleep because I knew that when I did some form of terror would dominate my dreams.

In one dream, a huge snake, bigger than a house, would chase me through the woods into a rickety old shack with a screen door. Sheer horror would freeze me to the far wall. It was a feeling of helplessness with no possible escape. The snake showed its fangs, and then pushed its forked tongue, dripping with saliva, through the holes in the screen and brushed across my face. The bones in my body ached and with every movement of the fiendish tongue I shrieked. The tongue would continue to coat my face with slime until I'd wake up.

Other times a gigantic rat as big as a six-foot man would chase me in a big room, corner me, and try to eat me. Somehow I changed places with the rat and had it cornered. I would hit the rat on its nose until I knocked it out. Once while married to Jack I was having this dream and, although asleep, thinking I was bopping the rat, I hit Jack in the groin. Jack woke up in pain, cursed, and was virtually immobile for several minutes. I did the same thing years later to my second husband, Allan. "Why did you do that?" he asked after shaking me awake. "I was trying to kill a huge rat," I replied. He said, "Well, I think you succeeded." He slept on his stomach after that.

In a small house there was a room with a mammoth white wall with no beginning or end. By the baseboard of that wall was a small mouse size hole. I would peep through the hole and see a rolling floor, like rolling hills and valleys. Each valley was covered with a deep, blood-red carpet. In each valley lay a member of my family, dead; Mom, Dad, Mary, Tish, Doris Lee, Ward, Bart, and Harry; also the priest. I could see myself walking on a level carpeted pathway from which I could view each of the bodies, making sure each was indeed dead. When I'd wake up I would be depressed knowing it was just a dream and all my tormentors were very much alive.

Another dream was of a large cathedral with lots of statues and stained-glass windows. Magnificent chandeliers sparkled with diamonds. Deep, royal blue carpet ran down the aisles. No one was in the seats but me. I observed this from a private balcony far above. People whose faces I could not see would be carrying beautiful gold and silver caskets. I could see the occupants in succession; Mom, Tish and Mary. All were clothed in finery of royalty. I would be feeling sad that they died yet glad that they were; all the while wondering how they were entitled to such an elaborate funeral. Was that a reward of being evil?

In another dream I would be going for a ride in a car with Mom. We would end up at a hospital where they drained all of the blood out of me so that Mom could have it because she did not have enough of her own. I would die, float around, and watch my family live without me. Mom rode away from the hospital in a horse-drawn hearse. I couldn't see the horses, but I could see the attendant who was holding the reins. The attendant was my dad. As I floated around I saw myself tugging at his arm and collar, screaming, "Why did you give her my blood? Please help me." It was like I was invisible as he never felt or heard me. I would wake up, then fall back asleep and dream it over and over again.

I am sleeping, feeling safe and at ease, when suddenly I sense that someone is in the doorway of my room. I look and see a large black shadow the size of a very large man. The form comes toward me. I try to scream but I am too petrified to get my scream to come out. This black shadow consumes me as evil energy and takes me to the devil's house of fire way deep in the earth. I'd wake up, usually crying, sensing the evil of the shadow in the room, yet glad I wasn't in hell burning up. This dream did not occur nearly as often as the others did.

Again, I am asleep in my dream being tortured and I don't know why. Like a double dream, I wake up from one dream only to realize these huge frogs the size of rabbits with razor-like teeth are gnawing on my hands and feet. They are eating away the flesh and bones. I can feel them crushing my bones. The pain is excruciating and wakes me up from both dreams. My hands are numb and tingling. I do not want to go back to sleep.

The eighth dream finds me in the front yard of our Ramsey home. I am walking across the lawn when, out of my peripheral vision to my right, there suddenly appears a tall grave marker. I look down to read it and my dad pops up out of the ground right in my face. I jump back and scream with horror. I feared that he was going to pull me into the grave with him.

As often as I had dreams about people being dead and wishing them dead, I believe that the Lord had a hand in me never actually making plans to carry out any related plan of action.

These nightmares stopped about three years into therapy.

The End for Mom

Mom worked during all of the twenty-two years she lived at Tish's house. During the first twelve of those years it was my job to go over there every Tuesday and clean, do dishes, laundry, gardening, clean the pool and shop areas, and other chores as requested. After my second divorce from Jack, I saw less and less of Mom over the next ten years.

It was in 1982, about six hours following artery surgery, that Mom had her stroke. She was seventy, over two hundred pounds, and diabetic. For most of the final years of her life she lived in nursing homes. She was paralyzed on her right side.

Mom died in 1987, gagging on her own vomit; death due to congestive heart failure.

During a visit with Mom I had confronted her about being such a hateful mother and causing so much pain in my life. She just gestured she didn't know anything about it, like nothing had ever happened; she put across the impression that she was guilty of doing nothing wrong.

Several visits later, while I was sitting on the edge of her bed and she was in a wheelchair, she put her left hand on top of my knee and made eye contact with me. She was mumbling in a way that sounded like she regretted something. "Are you trying to say you are sorry for the past things you have done to me?" I asked.

She nodded her head yes. I told her I had forgiven her because God asked me to so that I would not have hate in my heart. But, I said, "Take your hand off my leg. Your touch is still painful to me." She pulled back her hand and seemed to go inside herself.

I went from the nursing home to a nearby Catholic church and talked to the priest. I told him about Mom, that she was catholic but had hated God for over fifty years; that she might be dying and needed confession and last rites. He let me know later that week that he had seen her, that she took Communion, and they had a "real nice chat."

Shocked, I said, "What? You mean you chatted with her?"

"No," he said, "we chatted together."

"She talked to you . . . in words?"

"Yes. Why wouldn't she?"

"She hasn't talked to me or any of the family that I know of since her stroke five years ago," I said.

My first impulse was to rush to Mom and choke her. I did go over and confront her. It was a Wednesday morning during the close of worship service in the main dining room. They were singing *Amazing Grace*. I stood in the doorway and noticed that Mom's lips were synchronized to the words. I felt that the Lord was telling me that this was going to be a healing time for me and Mom. But before going into the room I saw her nurse who confirmed that Mom talked to her all the time. I went over to Mom's wheelchair, kneeled down facing her so that we could be eye-to-eye. As I began to sing the last verse of *Amazing Grace* her mouth stopped moving. When the song was over I said, "I understand you talk?"

She gave me a confused look and said, "I don't know." That was the one and only phrase I had heard her utter after the stroke.

"I know you talked to the priest and your nurse because they told me you did. I think it is cruel that you will talk to them but you won't talk to your children or grandchildren. What kind of sick game are you playing? It really hurts."

Again she uttered, "I don't know."

I turned and asked her friend, also in a wheelchair, "Does my mother talk to her nurse?"

"Yes, she does."

Turning back to my mother I said, "Mom, I love you very much but I don't like you. You are not a very nice person."

I took her good hand in mine, focused into her eyes which were like a deep black hole, and said, "Good-bye, Mom." I left with no intention of going back to see her again.

I did a lot of crying and soul searching after that visit.

Mom died three months later.

Part 3: The Road to Healing

Allan

I met Allan on his 18th birthday. Jack took me to the party, telling me that he was adopted by Allan's parents when his own parents were killed in that mid-air crash over the Grand Canyon involving TWA and American Airlines jets. Jack was telling lies and I was none the wiser. He still tells lies.

Truth Verses the Liar

When faced with a liar who twists truth to create self-doubt,
Question those liars, make their accountability come out.
Their bizarre behavior is a cunning diversion,
So as not to shed light on the truth and their perversion.
Stand fearless in knowing those liars will eventually derail,
We all know the truth, Gods' purpose shall prevail.

Allan looked like Elvis Presley and had baby-blue eyes. I was attracted to him, but he didn't make any advances to get to know me because I was his friend Jack's girl. Jack had been dating me a month already and Allan wouldn't risk interfering with anything Jack had going. It's only been in recent years that Allan told me that he was attracted to me at that first meeting.

As I described in Chapter 12, Jack and I got married after what could best be called a short courtship. I was desperate to get away from home.

If only Allan had interfered. Yes, that thought did cross my mind when I learned, over decades after the fact, of Allan's mutual feelings of attraction.

Allan got married many months after Jack and I did. He caught his wife in bed with another man and ended their marriage in 1971.

During Allan's divorce process his wife kicked him out of the house. He rented a room from Jack and me.

Then, when Allan got his house in the divorce settlement, Jack, our two daughters and I moved in with Allan and rented two rooms.

Jack began dating Allan's mom, who was old enough to be his mother. He moved in with her and they announced they were lovers. That along with his molesting our daughters clinched my resolve to file for our second divorce in 1972.

Allan let me stay, renting the two bedrooms and doing the house chores. A few months later I told him that I had found an apartment and would be moving out. He said he didn't want me to leave, that he wanted to have a relationship with me. I stayed, eventually moving into his bedroom. The girls now had their own rooms.

We lived together six years before we married in 1978. I felt it was wrong for Allan and me to live together outside of marriage. He wouldn't get married for such a long time because he didn't want to get hurt again like his first wife hurt him.

Allan is my rock; about 6′1″, broad shoulders, strong frame, black hair, and those baby-blue eyes that are soft, understanding, accepting, calming. He has a never-ending sense of humor. He is into me, sports and car racing.

For several years he operated Arizona Truck Specialties with his brother, whom we bought out in 1970. Allan and I were now partners in business as well as in marriage. He did metal fabricating, side panels for big rigs, and painted big rigs and horse trailers; he built trailers for semis.

I was the office manager and what I call the "left-hand man" in the shop, drilling holes and other tasks whenever Allan said, "Honey, do this."

We had a long-running battle over my desire to always keep things clean and neat. His attitude was, "Leave those things right there so I can find them when I need them."

The shop business survived until two major tool and equipment robberies led to financial woes and eventually vacating the building in 1992.

Allan now does body work on rigs for a major trucking company. His passion for me and sports has not faded. Nor has his sense of humor.

I could never have gotten through the five years of therapy without his support and understanding. He hadn't really known the mental anguish I'd been going through for so many years. I was tortured by the need to be set free from something very strong, deep, but I didn't know exactly what. I just knew I wanted to be free of it before I died. Many nights I paced the patio, cursing at God in anger, begging Him, pleading with Him. I wanted my children to know ME, not the person they thought they knew. I wanted them to love ME, even if I was sinful.

Then the dam burst in 1991, cascading the facts of my past in torrents upon Allan. He wanted to hunt my cousin Harry down like the animal he was in brutalizing me.

That Christmas, 1991, was one of hope for me. I counted my blessings as best I could and wrote the following prayer that special Holiday season:

Dear Lord,

I want to thank you for sending me Allan, a very caring, loving, and supportive friend, and husband. Thank you for Paula and Holly, two very different and very outstanding daughters. Thank you for special friends. Thank you for all those whom you have sent along the way to help me find my way to know the TRUTH, and for the ones who taught me to appreciate your love.

I especially want to take this time to honor my mother and dad for doing what they knew best at the time. The little love that they did give will live in my heart forever. No words could begin to express my gratitude for all that others did to deepen my appreciation for life and my love of God. Through them, God saw to it that I developed the ability to be ever so grateful for the simple things in life. A warm blanket, clean dry clothes, a drink of clean water, a warm bed, a bath, the smell of a bar of soap, eating unspoiled food, having the use of all my extremities... arms, legs, hands, eyes, organs; shelter from the elements, a kind word, a gentle touch, a moment's rest. Things that most people take for granted in life.

God knows I have come to appreciate what happened to me forty years ago as an anointing rather than a tragedy.

I wish to openly express that I am most grateful for the blood that is washing and cleansing my soul. I believe God has truly blessed me. His love will forever be my warm blanket to keep me from the cold.

As we begin to open these presents that He has so graciously given us, may we do so in a way so as to celebrate the birth of our dear Lord, the Son of God, Jesus Christ, the Almighty. Amen.

Scent the Past

Sensory recall is what the therapists would later tell me was what I had been experiencing. I only knew that strange things were happening. Some kind of tug-of-war was going on in my head between long-buried memories and a present steeped in denial. I was a basket case waiting to happen.

The catalyst to opening the door to my past was the Senate hearing involving Clarence Thomas (*later confirmed as the United States Supreme Court Justice*) and Anita Hill.

While watching the hearing on TV I heard a voice inside my head, way in the back of my brain, say, "They are giving so much attention to that woman because he said "long john dong" and now they are having a Senate hearing to resolve it. They would never tell on TV what happened to me."

Feelings of paranoia set in. A friend came by to help me sort my thoughts. "I keep smelling feces," I told her.

"I don't smell anything," she said.

Just days later, Allan drove me to Glendale Community College to register for the new semester. "Allan," I said, "roll down the window if you insist on farting."

"I didn't fart," he said.

"I have been smelling feces off and on since watching that hearing," I explained.

"It will probably go away," he assured.

But it did not go away. It got worse.

While standing at the financial aid office, about to sign the form, an attack of anxiety enveloped me. I began to tremble, and got weak in my knees. Allan took me to the counseling department.

A counselor immediately took us into his office. He asked me several questions. I don't remember what they were or what my answers were; however, I was very fearful. "Based upon your answers, you appear to be suffering from Post Trauma Stress Syndrome," he said.

It sounds like a description for some kind of brain defect or tumor, I thought, while verbalizing, "What is that?"

"Some people... soldiers, for example, and others who witness a violent incident or real bad car accident or some other trauma that they couldn't deal with emotionally at the time, develop a way of repressing those emotions so they can handle what is happened to them. Then later, perhaps even many years later, when they feel safely away from that trauma, those emotions begin to surface and cause some people to relive that trauma in their minds, like watching a motion picture."

He suggested that I see a counselor, Ron Bell, off campus who was known for successfully helping PTSS clients. I agreed to talk to the man on the phone before I would consider a face-to-face meeting. Feelings of mistrust welled up inside me.

While taking with Mr. Bell on the phone, I agreed to make an appointment, but only on the condition that I would be allowed to bring a friend. My trust level was below zero.

During the next few days I continued to smell feces and would for three or four months. Also, I began to have "flashes" of seeing myself as a little girl, about five, stripped naked, laying on my back with my legs bent over my head and a man penetrating his penis into my rectum. I also had flashes of that man penetrating my mouth with that same penis coated with feces.

It took three separate and independent professional opinions before I settled on Bell, a therapist I believed I could trust with all my past experiences.

Before I went for my first visit to Mr. Bell, I had also begun to smell burnt cookies, shellac, castor oil, motor oil, ether, garbage, rotten food, and vomit, all of which no one around me could smell.

What I was beginning to see and experience all over again, very emotionally, was "Horrors from Hell" in that place I called the "Numbness of Nowhere."

It was at this time in my life, in my mid-forties, that I seriously began the quest of "Looking for Closure."

Therapy

Ron Bell is of medium build, about five-feet-nine, sort of a sawed-off version of a young Clint Eastwood. He has sandy brown hair that tends to be more dark than not. Underlying his serious demeanor is a sense of humor that helps him keep things in balance.

In December, 1998, in response to questions I posed to Bell via e-mail to his one-year sabbatical base in South America, he provided this summary of meeting and treating me:

"I received a call from a colleague at the local community college who knew of my work with clients experiencing dissociative episodes. He said he had a student in his office who was so flooded with memories that she barely seemed in contact with reality. She didn't want to be hospitalized. It was a judgment call. I agreed to see her. The college counselor told me what she'd explained to him, that she was remembering being tortured by her adult cousin Harry when she was young.

"Barbara walked into my office accompanied by her friend, whom she'd brought for both moral support and physical safety. She didn't feel she could drive herself. Her trust level was nil. She asked where the restroom was, but had trouble following my directions, so I started walking her down the hall. She stopped abruptly and insisted I not accompany her. Everything occurring around her – including me – was triggering terrifying memories.

"Like her college counselor, I was concerned that she might require hospitalization. But first I hoped to establish some rapport and see if we couldn't stabilize her. Five minutes later I had my first working hypothesis. Someone as intelligent as Barbara was sure to acquire a DEM III and further inflame herself with the most damaging passages therein contained. Yes, she was exhibiting paranoia, hallucinations, and ideas of reference, rage, mania, and mood swings. But these symptoms could be used in any of a dozen diagnoses.

"Rather than diagnose, I prefer to formulate a working hypothesis and remain flexible enough to let it evolve rather than attempt to make the client conform. My hypothesis was that Barbara was communicating on a variety of levels, most of which were outside of her conscious control.

"My theoretic bent, if I have one, is that every part of a person, conscious and unconscious, is always attempting to do something useful. Issues arise when different parts attempt to help in ways which are not compatible. This typically stems from a lack of internal communication. Every physical symptom, every nonverbal sensation, be it auditory or visual, tactile or olfactory, can be viewed as an unconscious communication. Barbara was experiencing all of the above.

"Barbara's nonverbals indicated that a part of her believed it necessary to become consciously aware of long-buried memories – to what purpose it was not yet clear. Other parts believed this to be a disastrous course. I began a series of questions that could be answered either yes or no. I directed my questions to Barbara's unconscious parts, asked her to simply relay their answers as determined by strengthening or diminishing of her physical symptoms.

"Soon, Barbara was experiencing her unconscious parts auditorally. The parts agreed to a sorting of the flooding memories, selecting individual memories to resolve in a more orderly fashion.

"That first session lasted over two hours and involved at least part resolution of several memories. Barbara's internal parts, having experienced some healing, now had hope of further healing and agreed to slow the flooding and begin to work together. I suggested that the parts begin journalizing and write me letters as a way of letting their needs be known, and organizing the myriad memories and issues facing them.

"Barbara left the session with a different outlook, expressing great relief and some hope that the issues could be resolved. As important as any other result of the session was that Barbara felt that in some measure she had been heard, acknowledged, and believed. These issues of trust and validation would emerge frequently throughout the course of therapy as Barbara learned to validate herself.

"In the weeks, months, and years to come, Barbara went through predictable phases of hope and despair.

In psychodrama, therapy is often likened to the peeling of an onion. Barbara's onion had many layers. We often thought to have reached the final layer, only to discover a whole new sheaf.

"At times Barbara would appear to experience a recurrence of symptoms; but rather than view this as a backwards step, we looked at each symptom as another part's response to issues which previous parts had already resolved. Where one part may have experienced an event as terrifying, another may have felt her anger, another her shame, and still another a sadness for the perpetrator.

"Each feeling had its legitimate place in coming to terms with the abuse she experienced. Barbara's relationship to her parents was highly complicated, especially with her father who began as her hero, but was revealed to have been another perpetrator.

"Watching Barbara resolve her father-daughter conflict brought home to me the tremendous complexity of human relationships. It would have been convenient simply to paint him as the villain, vent her anger, and dismiss him. But to truly understand and validate herself, Barbara had to acknowledge and accept the part of herself that would not dismiss him, that had experienced other than cruelty at his hands.

"Likewise, it would have been convenient had the New Jersey police uncovered evidence of the crimes Barbara witnessed. Without this external validation, Barbara had to search deep within herself to uncover *just what validation meant to her, and what blocked her from that validation. It was a strange and painful blessing that she was given this challenge to know herself even more profoundly.*

"The final convenience would have been if Barbara's therapy had ended with a complete cessation of all symptoms and complaints. But as Barbara's experience shows, human beings are creature's far too profound, human relationships far too complex for nicely-packaged solutions.

"The duration and severity of Barbara's symptoms and the remarkable nature of their resolution afforded her entire family the opportunity to look inward. Other members of the family began their own therapeutic journey as a consequence of witnessing Barbara's healing.

"Resolution of dissociative experiences does not require an end to dissociation. Barbara remains in good contact with her parts when appropriate. She might agree that her dissociation no longer controls her; rather, Barbara now uses her dissociative abilities to lead a highly productive and satisfying life.

"Barbara made a courageous decision to enter therapy. To her credit, she persevered to the point where not only she personally but her entire family benefited. Hers is an important story which I'm honored to have been a part."

A flannel blanket was my constant companion to therapy sessions with Bell. I held it on my lap to cover my private areas. I always felt he could see through my clothes and so could other men. One time – three years into therapy – I forgot the blanket. Bell gave me a stuffed animal to hold on my lap.

He would lead me into a trance-like state so we could focus on a particular issue involving one of my inner selves. Over a period of time twelve distinct inner selves emerged with clearly individual personalities. These selves are what Bell referred to earlier in this chapter as my "unconscious parts." Each part or inner self conformed to a specific time period in my life. "Baby" was me until about age two. "Bobba Jean" was age two to three. "Butch" spanned the years three to five. "B.J.," who was a very tormented part, was age five to seven. Then there were "Cleo", seven and eight years old; "Princess", nine through twelve; "Gravel Voice," thirteen; "Babs", sixteen; "Barb", eighteen to twenty; "You Mom", who was married to Jack, ages twenty to twenty-two; "You", from twenty-two to twenty-eight; and "Barbara", from age twenty-eight on through the five years of therapy.

I would close my eyes and Bell would start telling me a story. "This is the story about a little girl who came to me for help. Where are you?"

"I'm right here," I'd say.

"Well, go deeper into yourself.....Are you there?"

Early on, I'd sometimes open my eyes and make sure he hadn't moved. "What are you doing?" he asked.

I told him and he said, "Well, you're building that trust."

Once my trust level built up, I easily went into trance and my inner selves began to communicate. But from the first sessions, I made my feelings clear that I believed in Jesus and wanted His name remembered and used before I would allow myself to enter anything resembling a trance or hypnotic state. Bell, being Catholic, agreed to this. I don't know how to explain it, but it was like I was led into a trance while still being aware of every-thing around me and what was going on. And my trust grew; however, I kept the flannel blanket as part of my routine in therapy sessions with Bell.

While on what often seemed like a hair-pin road to recovery, I also had therapy sessions with other professionals in one-to-one settings and also in groups. One of those professionals was a psychiatrist who confirmed Bell's assessment and who pre-scribed meds that helped me from following through on thoughts of suicide during periods of what seemed to me at the times as deep holes of regression.

My involvement in one Twelve Step-type group was short-lived. The group was led by a gay/incest victim survivor. After the third meeting at coffee she slid over close to me and caressed my shoulder with her hand. "Don't touch me like that," I said. "Don't touch me at all. This meeting is over." I left and never saw her again.

Another group was an inter-faith group which usually had eight to ten participants. It seemed quite shallow, like all the participants were spinning their wheels while staying entrenched in their own private ruts.

I did get valuable help from one-on-one sessions with a Christian counselor and with a Christian-based group.

The five years on the road to healing were at times a wild roller coaster ride; other times like waves of depression were going to engulf me. You will see what I mean as you read excerpts from my journals.

My Counselor

Feeling safe, knowing he's there, willing to help.

Greeting me at the threshold, walking the pathway,
guiding me from the beginning.

Addressing unsettled issues, recalling horrifying events,
identifying painful emotions, dissociating negative connections.

Exercising my weakened trust, from a wound inflicted
so long ago by lust,

Understanding, patiently encouraging me to grow,
one step at a time, my counselor.

Photos

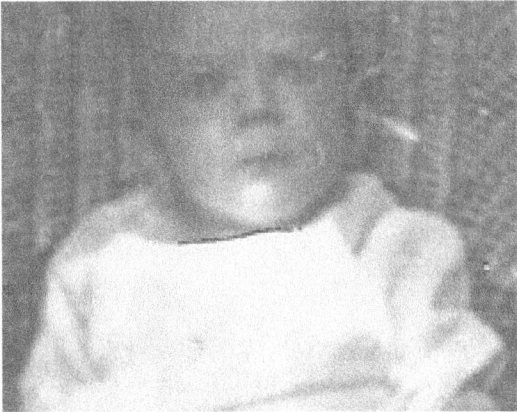

Me in wicker chair: I was about four (4) months old.

Me in baby stroller: I was about two (2), let to sit in the sun while mom did laundry.

Photo of me with arm across chest; hand on heart.

Me with a white head band in black and white dress. I was 18, it was May of 1963. My first husband and I conceived our first daughter that evening. I was very confused, anxious, felt used and unloved, but wasn't aware there was 'another life' waiting for me to discover.

A glossy of my acting portfolio photos. I did a few commercials; twenty-twenty eye care and Southwest Airlines. Also had a part in the movie, "The Grifters", but it was edited out at the end. For the first time, I felt pretty!

Me in my professional clown suit. I was about 30 in this picture. My clown name is Kismet... meaning Fate. I did clown appearances at the rehab clinic where my mom was following her stroke; birthday parties for friends and family; Halloween dress up that won contests. I clowned as part of my final exam in communication class at college, and did a clown eulogy for one of my best friend's funeral.

Me at my college graduation. I graduated with Honors; a 3.96 GPA. I was very proud of my accomplishments. I felt for the first time, I was not as stupid as I was told I was.

The ceramic heart with hand I made in ceramic class at college. A collection of what I saw at age 5 1/2 at Harry's after he plucked out Albin's eye; cut open Albin's chest and had me cut off Albin's fingers.

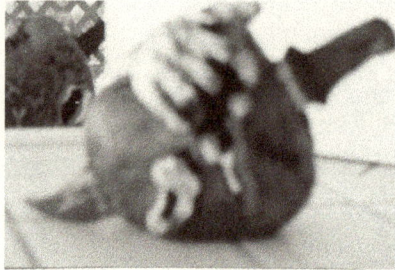

The Journals

Although some therapy sessions are so clear in my mind that they could've happened yesterday, others are shrouded in fog. Several months into therapy I began to write notes in journals so I could track my feelings and develop reference points along the road to healing.

7-15-92

I purchased this journal today to add another dimension to my healing. I haven't kept a journal since Mom found my diary when I was about ten years old. She read it and chewed me out, criticizing everything I wrote. She told me to "forget it" and that she never wanted to see me write anything again. ANYTHING. Then she burned it in the furnace.

7-16-92

Had a rough night, flashes of past incest; severe headaches. Saw Ron (*Bell*) today and walked through more memories in order to remove the painful emotions attached to those memories. Discussed B.J. not telling the whole truth and nothing but the truth, because of shame and how my older self needs to see B.J. has a reason for withholding the whole truth. She knows that her dad, mom, sisters, cousins and neighbors lied to her, were non-responsive, indifferent, inattentive, and evasive, preoccupied, didn't listen and were non-supportive. I needed to learn to recognize people who are good listeners, are supportive and genuinely care.

I feel like the only one who had my eyes open and showed true concern for what was going wrong in our family. Having a hard time accepting the fact that the rest of my family were in denial, weren't very nice people, and had no interest in facing any of the past family issues.

I am to learn to stay in the here and now; recognize when I dislike how people are treating me, and to express how I feel then and there, rather than suppressing my feelings.

7-20-92

For three hours during the evening, a child inside me was screaming to get out, without a sound, petrified. This went on for three days.

The Prisoner Within

Locked up in a cell, she continues to yell,
Nobody hears her, so she must be in hell.
There's an adult standing guard,
Hindering her escape.
A child's inside trying to get out,
Is anyone there?
Can you hear her desperate plea?
"Help me, help me find the key!"

7-23-92

Saw Ron today. I must eliminate panic as an option to handle my emotions.

When others invert and turn to denial, ask them "Are you kidding? If you are, STOP IT! I DON'T THINK IT'S FUNNY!"

Mom and Dad conditioned me and controlled me through fear. I feel rage heavy on my chest, arms; dead inside, hard, cold, stiff. I feel sad and angry. Abuse is all I knew as a child. What's to stop abuse in my old age? I feel like life is passing me by; I missed the golden ring; my space in life stands empty while I am into this psychological nightmare.

7-27-92

In therapy today I was allowed to metaphorically expel my anger by destroying my abusers in any fashion I chose. Afterward, instead of feeling relieved, I felt there was no safe place for me to be; felt exposed mentally and emotionally. Left feeling that the whole world is at a party and I am not invited.

7-31-92

I so want the New Jersey Police to find Albin's body and exhume it soon.

8-1-92

I wonder where I will end up. Although I feel that God is working through me, sometimes I believe that I have lost my mind.

8-5-92

Told Ron of the X marked on my forehead, belly and crotch with blood. Harry told me, "X marks the spot. It marks evil from Hell. Sex is evil... sex makes babies... they are evil. Your crotch is the snare of the Devil." I felt shame in my crotch. Ron said the Devil is a liar, will lie at all costs. Ron metaphorically washed the bloody X's off me with Holy water, asking Jesus to cleanse me of this evil and the lies.

8-10-92

Had flashback of my dad in a dream. Laying in bed, having my back tickled (*knowing this would lead to sex*), rolling over, having my nipples and crotch played with, lubricating, clitoral climax; feeling of being ripped apart upon his entry, words and hot breath in my ear; climax felt like being sucked and drained of self worth. Dad combing his hair; seeing his purple-pink penis. Afterwards, lots of degrading feelings.

8-12-92

Learned in group that I was always looking for solutions to everyone else's problems so I didn't have to feel my pain.... remembering I was not allowed to express my feelings without ridicule.

8-13-92

Having saved all these memories was inflicting pain. Discussed with Ron the need to let go of them by laying them at the cross for Jesus to burn and purify in the Holy fires. Recalled Mom telling me I was disgusting, dirty, and evil for masturbating. I saw her masturbate when I was two-and-a-half or three years old. Ron assured me this was how SHE felt about masturbation as a way to cover up her true feelings with this lie. Masturbating is really a natural part of growing up, part of self discovery.

8-18-92

Dear Lord, in the name of Jesus, your Son, my Lord and Savior, free me from these oppressive chains my parents and other grown-ups put upon my youth. AMEN.

8-19-92

Did a metaphor in which I burned down the library of incest memories, used the ashes for fertilizer, and built a Utopia for a safe haven for my inner selves that survived the horrors. Ron said these memories aren't doing anything bad to me anymore now that I have finally gotten to express them to someone who would listen and not discredit them.

The little girl inside felt fear at living without her past memories; never got to be just a kid; doesn't know how to let it go because she's too busy guarding her memories, her perpetrator's lies, and the fears those perpetrators instilled in her.

8-25-92

Had a dream in which I felt God had exorcised my body, mind and spirit of a lot of evil, vile feelings. Praise Him for that.

8-31-92

This evening I had a cry about Dad blocking my way to happiness. I remember thoughts of Daddy being on top of me, my wanting to go play and go to school, just to get off me and let me go.

9-23-92

Rough night. I remember screaming, "I don't want to be strong. I'm not able to handle this. Please stop." After calming, all I could think about was the question, "Why must there be so much pain related to learning?"

Since November 1, 1991 I have written fifty-one poems.

9-28-92

Very painful therapy session, talking about Dad and sex stuff and the drawings I did to depict what I remembered.

10-5-92

In therapy, talked of remembering rectal penetration, how I died emotionally upon entry until removal. Recalled Dad doing sex stuff to me on the way home from the bar he used to take me to. We were in his truck, waiting for a long train to pass. I cried when it went in, died and don't remember anything after that. Clickety clack, nine years old, why me?

I expressed feeling guilty, manipulated. Ron assured me that people who are caring and loving will not do that to you.

We metaphored going to God's glowing, where God could give me proper instruction about my female genitals; there I could learn that they were a gift from Him, not a curse. Ron said that as long as I won't place the blame back on my dad, I will wear it.

Allan told me he lost interest in porn magazines after he heard me tell of my past.

I hate falling to sleep; flashbacks of white probes, rectal and vaginal penetration, being observed and exposed; turning into a fat lady covered with spider webs.

10-19-92

Dreams with lots of noise, train, dog snapping at me, jump-starting my heart, lots of pain; picking up pieces that were the tips of Albin's fingers. I felt threatened and fearful.

Ron and I discussed that the reason my parents did those things to me was due to their own past problems and how they chose to deal with them. I recalled Dad doing sex stuff to me in the attic, basement, chicken coop and graveyard at the end of Grove Street. Dear Father God, it hurts not to matter and to be exploited by everyone who is supposed to love you.

There's a Hole in My Heart

There's a hole in my heart, where the rain gets in, no one can survive
the flood, not even the next of kin.

There's a hole in my heart, here comes the storm,

Quick, plug it up.

("Too late!")

There's a hole in my heart, behind the first beat, just to the left.

("Are you lost?")

There's a hole in my heart.

("Who cares.")

There's a hole in my heart, are you deaf, or am I dead?

I don't believe you've heard a word that I've said!

Take a look inside, can you see in the dark?

("What was that?")

There's a hole in my heart, damn it!

("OK!, I hear your cry, see you're in pain, I'm sensitive, I care, I'll
help you change your attitude, build up your trust,

Re-kindle the love that was lost.

With God's help, we'll fill up that hole, from the inside out,

Eliminating your fears and yourself doubt.")

("What's this, you're healing you say?

That's terrific, now can we go out and play?")

Emotional & Mental Trauma

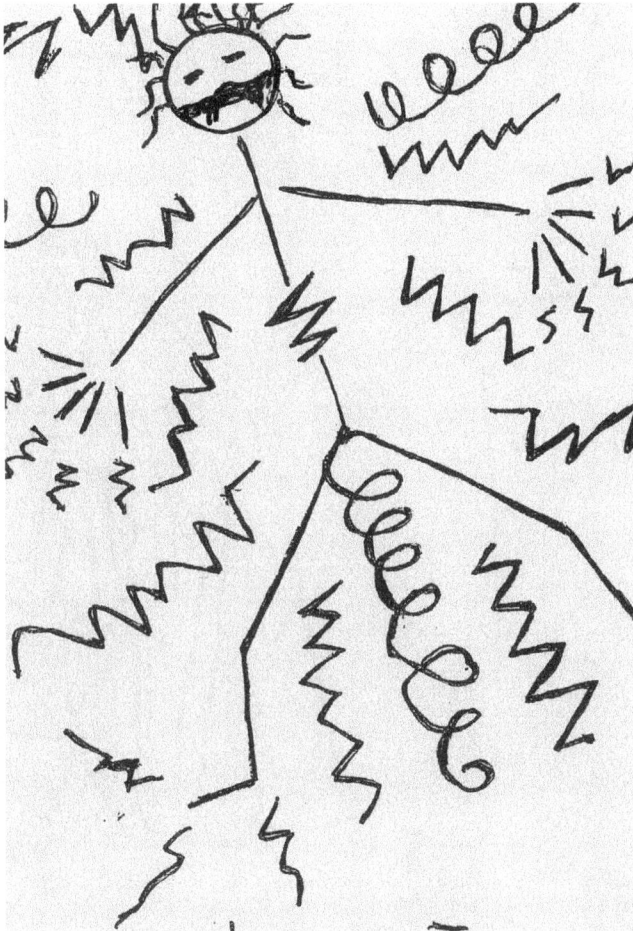

Dear Father God, it hurts not to matter and to be exploited by everyone who is supposed to love you.

Hanging at Harry's

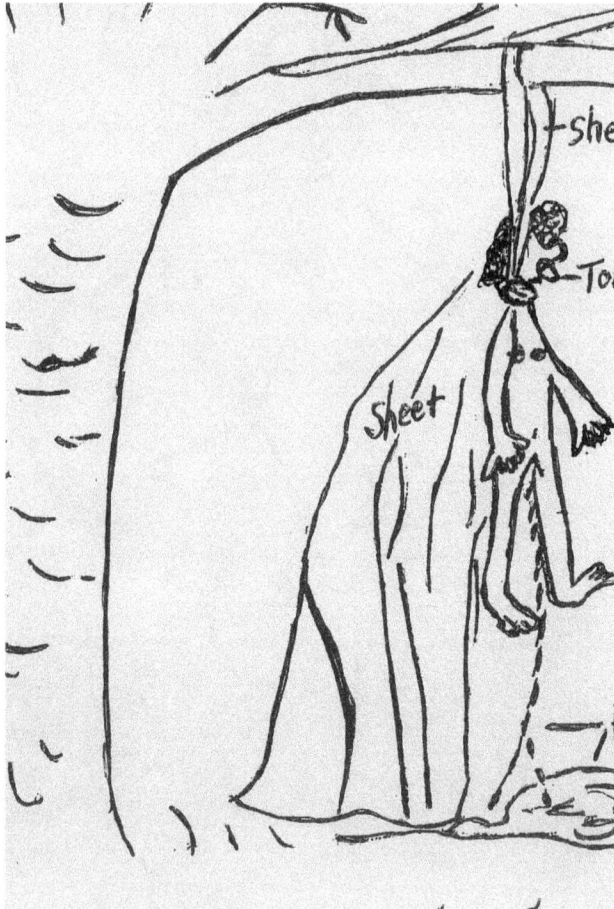

Harry quickly scrambled, still clutching me close to his chest into the house where he found a sheet. Back outside, he used the sheet to hang me from a tree limb. He and Amy watched as I jerked, squirmed, urinated and gagged for air. I had an orgasm, came face to face with God, and felt that I had literally left my painful little body. I believed I died.

11-2-92

Feeling lots of pain, gagging, wanting to die, hearing a voice from the past that kept asking, "You want this dick up your ass or down your throat?"

11-9-92

Worked with Ron in letting go of pain and anger. I was hanging between resistance and anger frozen deep; all the while wondering whether I am a miracle or born a curse to face death at every turn.

I DON'T WANT IT TO HURT TO BE TOUCHED ANYMORE! B.J. had a break through. She finally felt enough trust in Ron to feel safe enough to come out of shame and anger. Still hate my body, feel it's ugly and disgusting; I'm praying that God will show me how to overcome and see my body the way He intended. Yet I'm having feelings of dying, being separated from God, a lost soul.

12-8-92

Dream in which I see someone making crosses on my chest, lots of pain in back and neck. More gagging, choking, now someone scratching my chest with a cross.

12-14-92

Ron assured me I'm making strides in healing; not to be concerned with how fast, one step at a time.

Felt if I had been buried alive with Albin, I wouldn't be feeling this pain.

Remembered saying as a child, "God, please make the Devil stop hurting me" all over... over and over.

1-7-93

First visit with Church counselor. We talked about incest, rapes, molestations, and spiritual wounds. The work was directed at helping me clear up my confusion and the lies I was told about God and His Word. She said I had healed in leaps and bounds, that Ron was an excellent counselor. She said God was preparing me for service. I asked, "For what? When? Where?" I told her I had a trust issue with churches. We prayed.

1-11-93

During therapy vividly remembered being sodomized at 5-ish in the morning by Dad. I wanted to tell someone the truth before I died. That I didn't do anything wrong; it was Mom and Dad and Harry that did evil things to me. I called my dad God when he did sex stuff with me while thinking he was the Devil in disguise.

1-12-93

Went to group. Feel the counselor enables some of the girls to avoid their pain; that scares me, reminds me of my family dysfunction, anything to avoid the issues, truth and reality. I don't like it when others speak for me, like when one of the girls in the group said, "We are all fucked!" I told her, "Don't include me in that statement."

1-14-93

Worked with Ron on memories of being buried alive, hanged and ignored at Harry's. Very exhaustive session; reversing the guilt and pain onto the perpetrator. Feelings of being suffocated in the box, leaving my body while it was hanging, and seeing God and hearing Him tell me I had to go back into my body as He had plans for me. I became angry and told Ron, "What in the hell did He tell me that at five-and-a-half and not let me do anything for all this time?" I felt abandoned by God.

Suffication

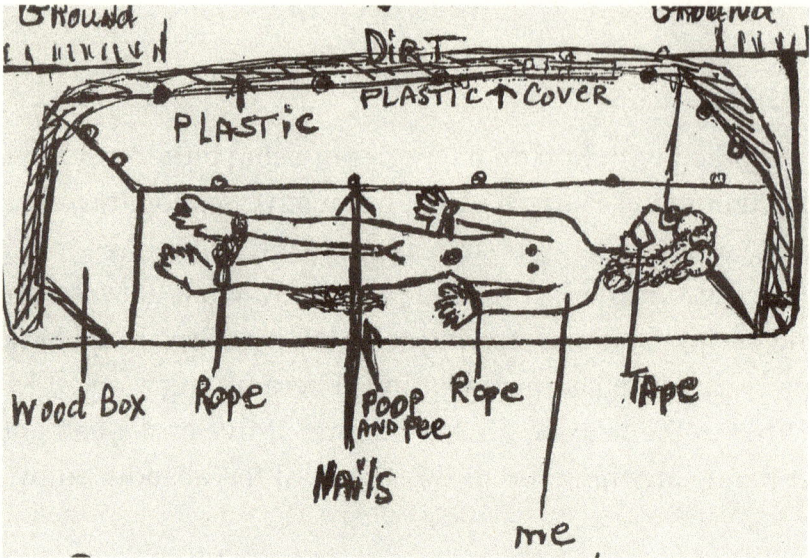

Harry built a box "just your size," he said. It was about four feet long, one-and-a-half feet wide, and one-foot high. He taped my mouth shut, tied my hands and feet, laid me face up in the box, nailed the lid on, and buried me in a hole, just inches deeper than the box was high.

1-19-93

Allan's touch is feeling better. I have been metaphorically directing my anger at my dad. I'm starting to realize that I am no longer living in the past; I am living in ME today, a healthy, loving, caring, nurturing adult who loves me and I take things one step at a time.

2-3-93

Detective Hernest called from New Jersey and asked me a lot of questions: who I told about this murder, who knew about it, how Allan responded, and wanted the names of my sisters. That scared me. Calling my sisters would only influence him to doubt me as they will do whatever it takes to keep this thing "buried."

2-11-93

Met with Ron. Recalled when Mom couldn't deal with my anger and placed my naked body, no shoes even, on the back stoop for a half-hour in the winter. I screamed and cried and yelled and begged. Also remembered Daddy having me take my clothes off in the basement and dance for him; bend over and let him hold my wee and put his finger between my vulva lips...the nicotine on his fingers burned. I left Ron's, sat in my car and cried, had a splitting headache, turned up the classical tapes to drown out the sobs like my mother used to do by loudly playing classical on the piano.

2-12-93

More nightmares reflecting on a Gumby clown I had at age six. Obsessed with masturbation, I transferred my affections onto this clown figure by placing it between my legs and using it to masturbate with. Because of poor hygiene by Mom, with me not being bathed regularly, my body smells transferred onto the figure. One morning Mom stuck it under my nose. "I know what you've been doing with this. You're disgusting, dirty, nasty, and I am burning this filthy thing." I ran after her to the basement, begging her not to throw it into the furnace, to wash it, and I wouldn't do it again. EVER. The clown went up in flames along with my attachment to it. Dad had bought it for me.

I am beginning to realize why I have no memories of my third-grade year. I believe that was when Dad graduated from playing with my privates to having intercourse with me.

Blood and Abandonment

Harry took me to a nearby pond and plunged me head first into it. The water was ice cold. He held me under until I began to take in water. He pulled me up and I'd grab and choke for air. He did this over and over until I lost all resistance to struggle. I felt a darkness coming over me and lost consciousness during this ordeal.

Abandoned

This evil won't let go,
Dragging me into depths of darkness, loneliness and despair,
Separating me from all I desire.

Consumed in its venom, scared, alone and without love.

Dear God, have you forgotten me?
Where's the love and joy you promised?

My own flesh and blood turned against me in my hour of need,
Afraid to weather the storm,
they ignored my deepest yearnings.

When their chips are down, they call out, "Gather-round",
Help me is their plea.

When my chips are down, they turn a deaf ear,
Put their rose colored glasses on,
Meticulously adjust their blinders,
So they won't have to see.
Once again leaving me,
Abandoned.

2-25-93

Told Ron that Mom used to get in my face and order me to just tell the truth. When I did, she beat me in the head and told me to stop lying; that my dad wouldn't do that and it didn't happen, and that's that. Period! So I believed "that" was true, so I wouldn't be lying when I said he didn't do what he did. Very confusing. Then I went upstairs and beat myself up, beating my head and stomach. I find it hard to accept and forgive when no one admits they have done anything wrong.

3-2-93

Visited the church counselor. By this time I had given names to several of my inner selves that experienced traumas while I grew up. One of them was Eight. The counselor and I agreed that Eight didn't know Jesus. She was frozen in time, totally separated. We prayed for Eight to reach out and touch Jesus' robe. I started crying; telling the counselor Eight was hiding behind Jesus' robe, afraid to come out.

3-4-93

In session with Ron, I finally realized why Eight had a hard time feeling safe and OK about being receptive to a hug. It hurt her, humiliated her to think she was getting just a hug and end up doing sex stuff.

3-16-93

Told church counselor that Eight was walking behind Christ, hanging onto His robe, dragging along unnoticed. Eight allowed herself to envision Christ touching her on the top of her head, ever so gently, to show her a safe touch from a man. We prayed. During the prayer I felt like a lightening bright light was flashing, transcending through me, like when I was in God's presence, when I died at age five-and-a-half.

3-25-93

Had clear recall of Dad coercing me into sexual activities, and me wanting to beat him up because of his actions, never discussing it with me, intimidating me with, "The roof over your head, food in your mouth, your education, the sweat of my brow." I just remember his hot wet hands, hot wet towel, burning upon re-entry, his shaving, putting our dog Rex into my bed, then leaving for work.

Upon penetration, it was like I would leave my body to escape the pain Dad was inflicting on me. There was a burning sensation as I re-entered my body at climax.

4-1-93

More memories flooded at therapy. Dad running his fingers through my hair; rubbing my face and genitals with his rough hands like sand paper; Eight with scissors in her hands, wanting to stab them into her own heart to kill the evil vampire inside her.

This was another time I couldn't just get in my car and leave. I had to sit in my car and wait to regain my sense of reality so I could drive safely.

Still having spells, dissociating, leaving my body, hating myself and my life, wanting it all to end.

I find myself in voice-stress rages over pent-up feelings of anger, and venting them at Allan, who understands he is not the focus for my rages, but a safe place to release them without fear of retaliation.

The subject of false memories is in the news. People are saying that psychologists are planting suggestive thoughts in their patients' minds. This scares me. By someone else's opinion, it would mean I didn't really experience what happened. It did happen; though I've wished many times that it hadn't.

4-8-93

I got embarrassed when Ron paid me a compliment. He told me that I was a leader, that I was courageous.

I believe I'm stuck in a memory of my dad having sex with me, the pain, and orgasm that I don't want to remember and can't seem to forget.

Ron said that since I allow myself to remember – should I choose to do so – I could then allow myself to forgive and forget; put the past behind me.

4-13-93

Today is a very special Jesus kind of day. Cody is being born today. While I was waiting at the hospital for Cody's birth, I visited the chapel to pray for Cody's foot to be normal and to guide the doctor's hands during the C-section. While sitting in the pew I felt like I was breaking and entering, committing a crime. Unespectedly, I heard the door knob jiggle and the creaking of hinges. A priest, dressed in black with a white collar, appeared. I panicked. My heart started to pound. I dashed out of the chapel to catch up with my other daughter on her way to the cafeteria. The priest followed me. I turned to go down the stairs. He followed one step behind me. I felt I was being overcome and he was undressing me, fondling me. I wanted to turn and start beating on his chest, claw at his face, and scream...STOP IT. GET YOUR HANDS OFF ME! SCREAM!!!!!!!! Instead, I pulled Paula, who was in front of me on the stairs, and got in front of her so she would be between the priest and me.

I knew later that I wasn't in my body, mind, hospital, but back in New Jersey on the corner of Cherry Lane, in the stone church as a girl. During a session with the church counselor, she said the incident at the hospital was used by God to validate my past molestation by a priest. We also talked about Scriptures, what it says about being married, obeying, and divorce. She assured me that no matter what partial truths my ex-husband used to deceive me, it was he who violated our marriage vows when he molested our daughters and committed adultery. It was his violations that released me from our marriage vows according to the word of Jesus. I realized that I needed long-term therapy.

4-15-93

Visited Ron and discovered that Eight has a name. It's Cleo. We discussed leaving God out of the session so Cleo could blow her stack. She felt set up and deceived and lied to.

I was so tired of being abused I remember saying; "I don't like it here. It's not fun. People are mean."

4-22-93

I worked with Ron. I told him Cleo felt that Jesus was a schizophrenic, an angel and the Devil in one. I dissociated and saw my bare genital lips, sticky with semen, felt Daddy kissing my neck, my toes curled tight, me jerking, flip-flopping like a fish, us both having heart attacks, but not dying.

It was happening over and over, leaving me sad, lonely, feeling dirty and ugly. It was so very painful to see Dad having turned into a Jeckle and Hyde, especially when he got drunk.

4-23-93

I called my aunt in Florida. She made my day. We talked about forty minutes. She told me that Mom's dad tried to rape her years ago. When she told Mom what had happened, Mom told my aunt, "The old fart still has it in him. Gotta give him credit."

My aunt said Dad was a coalman for the Pennsylvania Railroad when he met Mom's dad in a bar, and was later introduced to Mom. Dad's family was in a state of shock when they heard he was getting married--the wild-flying Dutchman settling down. My aunt said Dad was religious one day; mean as the Devil the next. **<u>She figured he molested all us girls</u>**.

Eanie Meanie Minee Moe

Eanie meanie minee moe, emotions tossing to and fro,
I see you've got a great big woe, eanie meanie minee moe.

Dad was sick from liquor. She said Mom was no prude and no angel, that everyone in Jersey knew she was having affairs behind Dad's back. She said Grandpa, Mom's dad, was a dirty old man.

I am at the point in my healing that I am glad I have come face-to-face with my past incest issues, even though at times it is very painful. I believe I can begin to live my life free from horror.

4-25-93

Nightmare last night. Told Mom to quit playing with my privates. She acted like she didn't know.

4-29-93

I told Ron that when I had flashbacks of sex with Dad I

would recognize his belt, buckle, Khaki pants, bare chest, and hands, but he had Jesus' head on.

We are working on me being able to separate fear from guilt and blame. Yet I find myself with so much frustration. Sometimes I am afraid to live and scared to die, but want to die.

5-6-93

In visit with Ron, I told him about voices telling me to razor my veins in my forearms long ways, to be found in a pool of blood in the tub so everyone will know I am not lying and let the pain out at the same time. Ron told me to see a psychiatrist so I could get medication to help me though this part of therapy.

5-14-93

Allan and I flew to New Jersey. When we got there I felt like a spy sneaking into town. It had been thirty-six years since I was there. I had some confusion about directions, but many things became familiar and I soon found my way. The stone church was the same, still gives me the creeps. Drove through the cemetery, remembering Daddy doing stuff to me when he was re-digging a grave to the left side of the storage shed. I didn't recognize my old house, because the current owners had added a section onto one end and moved the driveway. They were cordial, allowed me to look around. The only happy memories were of the deer that grazed our back yard and

Christmas when everyone was halfway pleasant. I chose not to see the basement; too many terror memories down there.

A lady I had known still lived up the street. She invited us in and verified many memories: Dad being mean, violent, and loud, as his voice echoed through the woods; me running to her a lot for safety; even still had a hot pad I knitted for her when I was eight. While visiting this lady, two old high school chums of Doris Lees' stopped by. They verified my remembering their neighbor being raped by her step-father, and were not shocked when I told them about Ward raping me in the shower.

Allan and I went to Oakland and drove right to Harry's old house, led only by memories in my head of being driven there as a kid. We also checked in with the Oakland police but Detective Conklin wasn't there. He had left town for the weekend. We spent the night in a nearby town.

We went to Harry's old place again. I told the renters I used to spend the night in that house with my cousins years ago. They let us in to walk through and reflect. Feelings swelled up inside me of fear, horror, disgust, murder. These renters were as filthy as Harry and his family was. The place looked the same.

We went to where Harry's widow lived. She said their daughter never got married; their son was gay, divorced and had a police record. I got her to verify that Harry was an alcoholic, the direction of the pond he tried to drown me in. She said, "I am not saying anything." Still hiding the lies and truths like a loyal trooper. She was very cold and distant. From there we drove to Pennsylvania to stay with some friends.

5-23-93

Church counselor agreed I should continue to take anti-anxiety medication until I got through this part of my therapy with Ron.

5-27-93

Don't remember much of session with Ron. Deeply suppressed; feelings of trauma from trip to Jersey. After the session my pulse was 60 beats per minute. I am feeling powerless again.

5-29-93

Cousin called, Dad's brother's kid visiting from California. He asked if he could come by. He shared that his dad and mine were very young when their dad died. Said their older brothers raised them, one being Harry's dad. He said as a young boy he'd been traumatized by Harry and one of Harry's brothers.

He confirmed that Harry had many rifles, shot at a kid, sodomized a horse, and got no nurturing as a child. Said my grandpa—Dad's dad—was shot in the stomach for having sex with a young girl. Said Dad had an affair with a married woman. He told me that Harry was hateful, mean, and perverse. When I shared my horrors at Harry's with him, my cousin broke down and said he didn't want to hear anymore. He said he believed Harry was trying to kill me. He got right in my face, eye-to-eye, and said, "I believe your dad did what you say he did to you."

My cousin's visit was short, but very validating for me.

Perpetrators call denial damage control.

6-1-93

Talked to Detective Hernest, who was curt, cutting me off in the middle of my statements, telling me he didn't give a damn about Harry as Harry is dead. He triggered a feeling within me that this was a man who possibly could be acting like I might expose one of his colleagues of getting rid of his retarded son, and not filing a missing person's report after Harry killed him. Some-times I feel I am in the middle of a bad movie, a murder mystery-horror flick, that keeps you spinning and dizzy, trying to figure out when the officials are going to WAKE UP AND SMELL THE COFFEE!

I called back again and again until I got connected to another detective, who was courteous and interested in what I had to say. I told him I felt there was a conspiracy within the Oakland Police Department at the time of the murder to cover the disappearance of the boy. He said he would pass the infor-mation along and wished me a good day.

6-3-93

Went to the psychiatrist's office to discuss getting medication to stop the desire to kill myself. I kept saying Phil. 4:13 (*I can do all things though Christ who strengthens Me.*) over and over in my head as I entered the office; a scared little person inside me clung to Jesus' right leg and He wrapped his robe around her to keep her safe during the visit.

The Dr. put me through a battery of tests, after which he said I was disassociating, experiencing anxiety, suffering from Post Trauma Syndrome, and had multiple personality dissociation. NOT LIKE SYBLE.

I left there feeling scathed, examined like a lab rat, halfway realizing I actually lived to give testimony of being incested, tortured, and involved in Harry murdering that boy.

The same day I saw Ron, cried all the way to his office. Accepting what I tried to forget, but couldn't, and realizing the truth was not a lie like my parents tried to convince me it was. All seemed so overwhelming for me to digest. I didn't know whether to be happy, terrified, or sad. Happy the truth was finally out of my archives of horrors. Terrified that "Someone" Harry had told me would kill me should I ever tell... might just do that. And sad, feeling sorry for myself as a little girl; sorry for Albin not getting a proper funeral, and sorry I didn't have loving parents.

When I got home I called my cousin in California. He said the detective called him, discounting anything he had to say not directly related to the murdered boy; telling my cousin he was discounting my credibility about the supposed crime due to my being in therapy.

That's the thanks I get for SURVIVING? I told myself, I did all I could, cooperated with the law, told them the boy's remains were under the duck pond in the back yard of Harry's old house; and prayed Albin wouldn't expect a five-and-a-half-year-old child to do more.

Ron helped me realize I didn't cause Harry to do those things to me. It was his drunken, enraged, and hateful behavior brought on by his own experiences, and it was Harry who hated God. Harry exposed me to his sick mind via Mom having an affair and me walking in on them.

6-7-93

Prayed with church counselor to have God direct Albin's ex-humming so I wouldn't have to carry the undue burden.

6-10-93

Took my Klonopin medication prior to seeing Ron. He didn't get into any painful areas so I could evaluate my control and relaxation from taking the meds.

6-12-93

Dream again about Allan leaving me for another woman and returning me back to my ex.

6-17-93

I told Ron that I am continually feeling everyone knows something I don't know. I missed the boat.

6-24-93

Took meds before seeing Ron. I would dissociate and try to project my dad onto Ron and deny I was doing that. It was obvious I was trying to verbally re-enact what I experienced as a child and Ron wouldn't allow me to do so. He directed my attention to working it out another way.

7-2-93

In the middle of the day... having dissociation. My nine-year-old memory is on her knees, repeating over and over, I did sex stuff with my dad. She is in church, crying to God, I'm disgusting, take me home, back to Heaven, or kill me for my evilness.

7-5-93

Don't quite remember this session with Ron. Maybe the meds. Left wanting to be with my Lord instead of this world.

7-6-93

Psychiatrist said I'm going through the most painful part of recovery: "Acceptance." He told me he knew how painful this process can be and to continue at a steady pace.

7-7-93

Church counselor told me I was making great progress. Recovery time for a "Wounded Child" is much longer than it is for major surgery. I told her I was told as a child that I was selfish, too sensitive, insistent, sulked too much, demanding, wicked and evil. She said those caregivers were evil to tell me such things and it simply wasn't true. The counselor said she would be moving to Colorado soon, that the Lord will show me how to separate the shame and blame and anoint Allan and me to fall in love all over again, only this time without incestual pain.

For months now I've been going to aerobics class which is burning off my depression but not doing a thing for my weight.

Dream about snake under my bed, my eight-year-old crying, in Mom and Dad's bedroom, being ignored, them acting like I was sick and a spoiled brat. How could Dad do this and act like he didn't do anything, act like he didn't know why I was in so much pain? He was really evil and didn't love me. He didn't know how.

7-13-93

Nightmare. Shower experience, being raped by Ward, soapy, wet. Deafening scream woke me and Allan.

7-14-93

Nightmare. Sex with the devil, an ugly, snaggle-tooth balding man, and he poked his fingers in and out of my genitals.

Went to last visit with church counselor. She assured me I was her hero. Said there is a difference between guilt and shame. Guilt is when you know you did wrong. Shame is when you didn't do wrong, but think you did.

7-15-93

Took meds, cried on the way to Ron's office, asking Jesus to take the shame from me, show me how to let it go.

Learning to live without my dad.

JESUS.... PLEASE SAVE MY SOUL.

7-24-93

Had that same dream about Allan leaving me for another woman. Making me feel like a little girl without any say about it.

7-26-93

Ron used metaphor of being in a movie theater, me in the seat watching the movie, another me in the projection room watching me in the seat and in the movie. I began to lose sight in my left eye, but could see out of my right eye. Very sad, back and forth in the air, I disappear in light rays to leaves on the trees and snowflakes. I realized that what I was seeing on the screen was me and Dad having sex. I did lots of crying for about twenty minutes of the session. Ron said I was brave and did good to allow myself to see the truth and set myself free.

On the way home I prayed to God to sanctify and free my body, mind and soul. I didn't even know what sanctify meant; had to look it up in the dictionary when I got home.

8-22-93

For days now, I feel like I am in mourning. Depressed. Every Sunday since 1982 Allan and I take three-hour fast walks to rid ourselves of stress and exercise our hearts. Thank God it is Sunday.

I feel the thing I need most is love. Little girls' arms are made of love, not moth powder.

My intimacy days with Allan are still on hold. I told him I didn't blame him if he wanted a divorce so he could marry someone without this kind of background. Allan said he is patient, this too shall pass and we will once again be romantic and intimate, only this time it will be even better, no past issues intruding anymore. He assured me he loved me.

8-30-93

Talked with Ron about recent pap smear, being embarrassed, triggering memories of Dad fingering me, having me suck on his penis, down in the basement by the work bench; then he drank his beer and told me to get the hell out of his sight. Mom took me to Dr. Hawse and had me lie, tell him I had injured myself in my bottom and wee. She told me not to tell the Dr. the truth or Mommy would be beaten up by Daddy. Mom and Dr. acted like I was the one with the problem; Mom doing

~ 164 ~

things to my bottom so no one would know about Dad doing it to me.

Shame, sadness, anger overwhelmed me.

9-13-93

Woke up middle of night crying. Dream. Allan leaving me for a younger, sexier, richer, thinner woman. This time I saw her hair. It was red. Her name was Shannel. I don't know why I keep having these dreams about Allan leaving me, but I know they make me real sad, broken hearted.

9-18-93

Art class. Drawing fingers. Remember being forced to chop Albin's fingers off.

9-23-93

Took meds and saw Ron. Told him our medical expenses were increasing as we spoke...paying/owing him, the psychiatrist, group, medications. I felt a very deep desire to die and go live with Jesus. THIS IS NOT LIVING! Another part of me felt the Devil was trying to get me to kill myself. I am in so much emotional pain.

9-25-93

Went to a Catholic church to talk to the priest. Told him about Dad's sexual abuses, the priest in Jersey, Mom, and other abuses. He said forty-one years of layered anger might take years of therapy to get over. While I was talking to this priest, I remembered another priest who disturbed me. It was in Avondale. I was eleven. I went to confession and the priest told me I was created by God to be a child bearer and to learn to be submissive to the male gender. He said my dad was teaching me how to be a woman. He told me to undress and he would come into the booth to see if my dad had done a good job. I ran out of that church as fast as my legs could carry me, my heart pounding, feeling like I was being smothered.

10-3-93

Still attending Christian survivors group.

10-15-93

Went for second visit with Catholic priest. He said the priest who molested me was a disobedient servant and lied to me about being cursed Catholic. This priest released me from being Catholic, said it was a matter of choice.

10-25-93

Saw Ron. Still lots of dissociating, projecting. Bothered by the Latin mumbo jumbo the 1950's priest used to curse me Catholic for life.

Started taking thyroid pills, .25 mg. Feel headache, irritable, very sensitive to noise. Feeling like I've had an overdose of caffeine, unable to cope.

11-2-93

Read six of my poems at support group as a way of sharing past issues. Several of the girls identified with some of the emotions in the poems. Didn't get much accomplished besides airing my fears.

11-8-93

When I'm on Klonopin I don't remember much of what the sessions with Ron are about, just a lot of emotional pain and crying. B.J. feels safe enough to come out of hiding in the dark when she is in Ron's office.

11-9-93

Went to group. B.J. came out there, too. She said she honored her parents to please God, but she honored them with a heart hardened with anger. We prayed for healing. I mentioned that while nursing Dad on his death bed, B.J. wanted to stab him in the heart.

I wrote Mike Wallace at 60 Minutes about Albin's murder.

11-22-93

B.J. told Ron she believes that she makes bad things happen because of the evil spell Harry and the priest put on her, and her having sex with her dad.

12-20-93

Visit Ron. Felt dirty from all the sex stuff memories. Ron had me metaphor, put on a new dress and leave behind the past and move on; wash away the sadness, shame, pain, suffering, anger.

12-21-93

Tried a survivors group at a different church, a twelve-step program. Felt it was cold, clinical, and ritualistic. It triggered fear, anger, and panic in me. Once out the door I ran, gasping with the sounds of screaming inside my head, to my car. What happened at this church? Why the fear? I prefer a group with opening prayer and references to Scriptures to address abuse issues.

12-23-93

Nightmare. Eight years old, hiding under my bed. He's pulling and grabbing my legs, a knife is in his hand. Woke up crying.

12-27-93

Rough session with Ron. A knife, headstones, stabbings, smashing, anger, sadness, under the bed, fear. Draining.

1-3-94

Cried in shower. All I want is to be loved for me, not my body.

1-7-94

Went to cemetery and put incest plaques on my parents' graves. Wrote on the plaques what I felt about what they did to me.

1-24-94

Allan and I went together to see Ron; discuss our awkwardness with sex since the recall of my past.

1-26-94

Allan visits Ron.

1-28-94

Woke up screaming from a nightmare like I've done many nights.

1-31-94

Saw Ron. B.J. split into two different emotions. We will talk to the angry one next week. I still feel overwhelmed, abused, tortured, hear screaming inside my head. I fear what will happen if I don't comprehend what it is I am too stupid to understand. Why didn't anyone tell me what was happening to me so I wouldn't be so confused?

2-9-94

Visit to Ron. Made good progress. Ron got information from both B.J.'s to help me face my anger, which was partly due to being manipulated and controlled by a sick adult. I told Ron I realize that I am getting better. He said that was good.

3-2-94

Explored my feelings with Ron about being raped by Ward in the shower, my fear, anger and belief in the nasty, cruel, insulting, vulgar things Ward called me while he slapped me and pulled my hair, holding my head and face. Forty years I feared taking a shower, waiting for the intrusion of a rapist, not realizing I was projecting from an incident that happened to me so long ago. Ron had a special part of me metaphorically get into the shower with me and tell me this rape is a thing of the past, that I am not a slut, was never a slut. The truth is I was violated sexually. That never made me a slut, only violated by evil doings by evil-minded people.

3-3-94

Stressful visit with Ron, who had to help me calm myself down. I metaphored going to the woods, near the brook, and a great earthquake destroyed my NJ home and the earth swallowed it up along with my family. I felt safe, concerned only about food and clothes.

4-5-94

Math class causes me to feel stressed and I hear a voice inside my head. PLEASE... GOD... JESUS... LORD... HOLY SPIRIT... LET ME DIE... I WANT TO GO HOME AND BE WITH GOD AGAIN AND NEVER COME BACK. Sometimes this voice is so loud that I think people close to me can hear it.

4-8-94

Psychiatrist says I need to take Moban to stop the intruding voice that wants me to die. He didn't want me to hurt myself.

4-13-94

I told Ron I was going to fly away with a white dove to be with God.

5-4-94

After three frustrating sessions, I told Ron that I was a lost cause. He said he didn't believe that to be true. I told him I was glad I had him to talk to and hated going at the same time. Talked about Harry's face; B.J. hanging, being dead, leaving her painful body and talking with God in the white, peaceful glow; then being rescued from hanging only to come back into my body to face more torture.

5-9-94

Still having nightmares. Fogged by the Moban drug.

5-11-94

Talked to Ron about freeing B.J. from hanging for forty-five-years, Harry and his evil face in mine, my fears of facing each day, and about anxiety associated with not getting to exhume Albin's remains. The session ended. My hour was up. Will continue next session. When I left; I felt like a cheap fuck being used by the hour. Only instead of me being paid, I got to pay. Hated it.

5-18-94

Happy Birthday to me. I turned forty-nine today and got to go to therapy because my dad decided to violate me and screw up my life. Left Ron feeling suicidal. Drove the car into a curb, hoping to flip the car over and kill myself. The car didn't flip. I figured God didn't want me and the Devil needed to keep me here, a hell on earth, for doing what I did with Dad.

5-25-94

At Ron's office, we set aside Dad issue and concentrated on Harry issue.

5-28-94

I had a job for two weeks, cashiering in a Hallmark store, until the older gal, who had gone to the same survivors' group, came in and exposed my past. The owner was bothered by this. I didn't work there anymore. Once again the past was destroying my future. WHEN WILL THIS END?

6-8-94

Ron used metaphor of turning my past into dust and putting it into Noah's Ark for God to tend to it.

6-10-94

Part of me feels Ron used me to get money. Another part feels I lived through some atrocious experiences and because of my love of God, He saw to it that I didn't die, but to become a representative for His cause. I still want Albin's remains exhumed and Harry's wife to pay for her part in the murder.

6-21-94

Psychiatrist released me with the option to refill my meds if I needed to.

Visited Ron. Talked about my feeling conjured, tricked, yet healing. Began to cry, I want my daddy. Remembered dancing with Daddy, standing on top of his shoes as he danced, holding my hands, to the Blue Danube Waltz. B.J. never wanted that memory to end.

I told Ron that I would never forget him, his God-given therapeutic talents and how he has helped during my healing. We discussed spending some upcoming sessions on current-day issues that the past has created, such as my weight gain, interrupted intimacy with Allan, relationship with my daughters.

8-8-94

Dreamed about my ex, realized his behavior was his issue, not mine. Forgave him. Made peace with myself.

8-31-94

Bradshaw says, "Abusive parents break the spirit in the child early so the child won't expose them."

Ron told me all the messages from my inner children are positive, and to remember they're trying to help me.

9-28-94

Talked with Ron about my anxiety with Algebra, how it triggers memories of incest and torture at Harry's. We worked out a plan to have me sing a song, inside my head, when ever this started to happen. I chose to sing "There's No Business Like Show Business" by Ethel Merman. It seemed to work. We also talked about my Sixth Grader destroying her dad, stuffing him into a coffee can and putting it in the kitchen on the Ark for safe keeping.

10-5-94

I recalled when I started to develop breasts and pubic hair at age eleven, grade six; Daddy raped me because I didn't want to submit to his incest abuse anymore. I wanted to save my "womanly" self for someone special – my husband. I wanted him to hurry, to get it over with. Ron had me metaphor burning down the house, putting Daddy's penis and testicles into a vice, pulverizing them and washing all the memory away with a melting snowball. Immediately after metaphoring, I dry heaved for several minutes and vomited into a trash can. I felt like the exorcist.

10-26-94

Ron said I was causing my own anxiety, reminded me I was no longer being sexually or emotionally abused – only in my mind, from memories. I told him I knew that, but didn't know how to stop doing it. He said we would devise a plan that would be acceptable to all my inner memory people and set it into motion in a few visits.

11-2-94

One called Gravel Voice, age thirteen, spoke out. Her dad finally quit having intercourse when she turned thirteen-and-a-half, when she started menstruation. The next two years he had me perform oral sex, deep throat, swallow his sperm, she would count the swallows. I had lots of jaw and neck pain, gagging reflex, stomach pain, and lots of anger. God's specialness inside me in a place called "The Nightingale" gave me the will to live, reminding her how He gave His only son to save her from damnation, Satan's lies and evilness.

When I was young, I would lie in bed and fantasize about flying on an eagle's back, far away from where we lived, with the wind in my face and the safe feeling the eagle gave me.

11-8-94

Did a lot of crying at Ron's. Loud screaming inside my head. Cried about Mom denying my physical and emotional pain and twisting my arm to stop crying about it; putting her foot on my chest and not letting me up, until I stopped. I told her I don't want to die yet. I want to be a testimony to the Lord so others will follow His beacon of light. Mom told me, "Never say that in my house again or you will die."

11-16-94

Had a real up visit with Ron. No tension. Only visiting a Utopia I created for my inner kids. We discussed a plan of action for me to use when I felt panic. First, to calm myself with slow breathing; second, to call a friend and say, "This, too, shall pass."

11-23-94

Went to Ron's. Discussed low self-esteem influenced by my sister Tish. We metaphored on *Alice In Wonderland*, eating grow and shrink crackers. I ate the grow crackers and Tish ate the shrink crackers, leaving me in the superior position in control of my own feelings.

3-24-95

At Ron's, remembering total uninhibited pleasure, feeling special during sex play with Dad... <u>before</u> Mom caught us in the act on the freezer in the basement; me, five; Daddy, forty-one. shame, guilt, anger grabbed me. That's when Mom's actions started revealing her hatred for me. Like everything was my evil, pre-meditated idea. Ron showed me that much of my emotional pain grew out of my feeling of total rejection by Mom. But much of my physical pain through the years was a result of Dad's continued sexual demands on me.

4-14-95

After Psychology class, I came home and called my sisters Mary and Doris Lee. It was part of a mini assignment on healing relationships through forgiveness. I hoped for a miracle. Instead, I got rejection, anger, blame. Doris Lee said I was years too late and hung up. Mary gave me an ultimatum: "Put this incest issue to rest or no relationship between us is possible." Her voice grew angry. She ranted and raved, "It never happened to me. It's too late to prove anything. You need to let go of this. I don't need your crap in my life right now." She raged on. Hanging up, I felt hurt, but not devastated. I had grown and was fortified by self-forgiveness.

4-19-95

Told Ron about my feelings after calling my sisters and their rejecting my appeal to start over. I metaphorically held funerals and buried Mary, Doris Lee and Tish in God's cemetery.

6-7-95

B.J. told Ron she was free at last and wanted to stop therapy with the option to call if I needed him. He agreed.

Keeper of the Light

Keeper of the light shining ever so bright,

("Who goes there?")

Tis "I," a shadow in the night.

("Step forward, let me see your face, tell me what you do?")

I go here and there without being seen,

Carrying messages all about your dreams.

("Douse that light! You'll reveal me, peel the paint off the wall,

Leaving no more art in sight!")

You're not making any sense, you're as high as a kite!

("No, I'm the keeper of the light!")

The View from Here

Now when I feel that I am in a box canyon emotionally, I turn to God, pray and wait for some direction.

No longer am I in a state of muddled fog like I was.

My journals were a mish mash at times; how-ever, the excerpts I've given you in the previous chapter should give you a feeling of the emotional roller coaster I was on.

I have learned from reflecting on my past that it does not own me or dictate who I am.

God has shown me how to refuse to let what has happened limit me from living a happy life. My confidence is based on my faith in God.

Grandma Hutton used to sing this song to me:

"Oh to da daze en da buslin an a bloom. Pray tell eve-body-z-don-gone ta da moon. Singin and a dansin... dem righteous folk sey... da bes thin ta do is gets down on yo nees an pray. I'm a bustin out all ova... an a rolin in de clova. He done sets me straight... I dun passed fru dem pearlie gates. Just like in dem days of ol... He be a lovin each an eve one of dem da soles. Doan eve let em douse yo light... doan matta if-en-yo black o white... in Jesus' eyes we all infinite. Yo is one of da special chillun... one of God's infinite angels... an don a yo eva foget dat chil."

I told Grandma Hutton what Harry did to me. She said, "Trus in da Lord... He be lookin ova evathin and evabody... He loves ya... Jesus loves ya... das all dat matters chil."

That humble lady who loved the Lord is one of my good memories. And, somehow, I sense she is one of the reasons why I'm alive today; a very good reason why the view from here is of a positive future for my life.

Amen.

Safe in Jesus' Arms

Now when I feel that I am in a box canyon emotionally,
I turn to God, pray and wait for some direction.

To Know the Difference

Hate, jealousy, anger, resentment, indifference, and loneliness,
To know the difference is love!

Epilogue

Several months into therapy, my youngest daughter, Holly encouraged me to call Harry and confront him.

I did.

Harry answered. I explained who I was and verified who he was.

"I remember what you did to me," I said firmly and calmly.

"You know what you did. Amy knows. Your children know. I know. God knows. And now the police know; I told them."

"Why don't you tell me all about it?" His voice was high-pitched sounding.

"It's too painful to talk about. I will pray that God will have mercy on your soul."

He hung up.

What immediately followed seemed like an exorcism. My body jerked and suddenly fell limp on the kitchen table.

"Are you OK?" my daughter asked.

"It feels like some evil has left my body," I said.

An aunt from Florida told me of Harry's death – heart attack just days after I called him. He was seventy-two. The Oakland police verified this report.

Part of me was glad he got what he deserved. Another part was enraged and felt like he had gotten away with his crimes, escaping the law and imprisonment. But, I did get to confront him before he died. That was very important in the healing process.

I found closure for myself; and continued to pray for Albin. His closure rests in the hands of the New Jersey authorities; those with the power to have Albin's remains exhumed from under the cement pond that sits undisturbed in the back yard where Harry and Amy lived

Collection of Poetry

Fear

Fear is the lion I ride,
To distance places from where I feel safe.

It's roar so loud and demanding,
My inner voice can't be heard.

This lion named "fear" runs swiftly,
Defending my speech, confusing my mind.

The ride's emotionally draining,
It leaves me feeling condemned.

As I begin to dismount, questions come into my head,
What are "my" needs, how do "I" feel, what is real?

Soon, I begin to believe in myself,
as I looked at the lion's true nature,

False Evidence Appearing Real.

Denial

What's this thing I can't see, hear, or feel,
Where does it get its strength?

It keeps me in such darkness,
Blinding my mind, concealing what's real.

It won't step forward or give me its name,
Or tell me from whence it came.

It claims authority to rob me of what's rightfully mine,
While it keeps me imprisoned and under painful restraints.

It's now so obvious; it could only have one name,
It's called - **"DENIAL"**

Communication

Communication, that's the key,
Communicate and you will see

Speak your heart!
Talk your line!

Communicate and you will find,
You too can have peace of mind.

Remember, instead of being caught up in self-pity,
Communication is the key to your "inner city!"

Reach In! Grab On!

Next time you're down and feelin like a clown,
Reach in! Grab on! Accelerate your mind!

Detach your "thoughts" from the negatives,
They keep you wondering why and how,

Attach your "thoughts" to the positive,
They'll bring you to the here and now.

It's the only place to be,
While you're reaching for your individuality.

Reach in! Grab on!

Truth Verses the Liar

When faced with a liar who twists truth to create self-doubt,
Question those liars, make their accountability come out.

Their bizarre behavior is a cunning diversion,
So as not to shed light on the truth and their perversion.

Stand fearless in knowing those liars will eventually derail,
We all know the truth, Gods' purpose shall prevail.

What's Happening?

Children are Gods' way of renewing life, so they say.

Is the world coming to an end?
What's happening?

Love one another, God said.

Broken pieces being thrown away, as though love were dead.
What's happening?

Love is Gods' nature, truth is His way.

Hate, lies, deception, causing such havoc and dismay.
What's happening?

The Prisoner Within

Locked up in a cell, she continues to yell,
Nobody hears her, so she must be in hell.

There's an adult standing guard,
Hindering her escape.

A child's inside trying to get out,
Is anyone there?

Can you hear her desperate plea?

"Help me, help me find the key!"

Pain Verses the Unfamiliar

Fragmenting again, unable to withstand.

No definite direction, no place to go.

Broken into shattered pieces, scattered,
with no form of my own.

Left here alone, in the depths of numbness.

Blown Away

Discarded with no love,
Seized by weakness, I collapsed.

Knees scraping the ground, exhausted from oppression,
Scathed by ridicule, wondering,
Am I to blame?

Blown away, I began to pray,
God, "PLEASE" help me, I can bear no more.
Lift me up; lead me away from this affliction,
Ascend me from this adversity.

Humbly, patiently, I wait.

Vile Knowledge

In a snake pit, consumed in fear; waiting for its bite.
Death comes not, and leaves me here, in pain to wonder.

Suddenly, one crawls inside me, entering through my nostril,
Forcing me to swallow.

Once ingested, the bile quickly eats away,
Deteriorating its flesh.

Have I just been nourished?
No, only compelled to vomit, to eat it once again,
Until it becomes a part of me and readies me for more.

"Vile Knowledge"

Suddenly

Suddenly, oh God, it's so final.

Now what?

Suddenly, oh God, face with no flesh.

Please don't!

Suddenly, oh dear God,

Please stop!

Picking up pieces, chop, chop, chop.

Suddenly, oh my God, tasting what beats no more.

What's next?

Suddenly, forcefully, lusting with death.

It's time?

Suddenly, pouring in the cement, burying the sin.

Pay attention!

Suddenly, hearing his threatening commands,
blocking it all out.

Suddenly, lies and fear carry a lot of clout.

Emotional Injury

Hard to see with the naked eye, easily concealed behind fear,
Severed heartstrings go unnoticed.

Afraid to view the damage, many turn away,
Others often jab and rub where it hurts.

Some say it's no big deal,
So long as it's not contagious.

Keeping their distance, refusing to accept it's existence,
Ignorantly labeling it, "weird", "crazy", "mentally ill".

Individuals alienating my feelings strikes deep,
Dishonoring my excruciating pain.

Withholding benevolence and appropriate affections,
Duplicating my emotional injury

Abandoned

This evil won't let go,
Dragging me into depths of darkness, loneliness and despair,
Separating me from all I desire.

Consumed in its venom, scared, alone and without love.

Dear God, have you forgotten me?
Where's the love and joy you promised?

My own flesh and blood turned against me in my hour of need,
Afraid to weather the storm,
they ignored my deepest yearnings.

When their chips are down, they call out, "Gather-round",
Help me is their plea.

When my chips are down, they turn a deaf ear,
Put their rose colored glasses on,
Meticulously adjust their blinders,
So they won't have to see.
Once again leaving me,
Abandoned.

Too Close to the Sun

A peaceful little planet in a vast universe,
A heavenly body called Princess evolves,
Too close to the sun.

His warm rays penetrate her environment,
causing a tingling within her ozone,
Circling around her, etching ever closer,
She begins to feel the heat.

Soon she faces the radiation head on,
Perspiration oozing, covering her entire surface,
Dear God, is she melting?

Etching nearer, bright beams blind her,
Feeling the fervor in the combustion, she disintegrates.

She got too close to the sun!

Silently in the Dark

Waiting in her twilight state,
Unexpectedly she was alerted by his lascivious
manipulative touch,
Silently in the dark.

Quiet as a church mouse,
She endures his carnal acts, while observed by another,
Silently in the dark.

Shame interact with pleasure,
Pain wrenched at her emotions while she
submitted with obedience,
Silently in the dark.

She felt like a nasty exhibition,
Raptured into sharp edged pieces that severed her love,
Silently in the dark.

Mortified, shrouded with guilt, nausea and
confusion submerged her,
Silently in the dark.

In an ocean of tears, once again, she lay lamenting,
Silently in the dark.

Sex at Five-And-A-Half

Vengeful eyes behind the physical thrust,
All driven by a demon called lust.

Ecstasy that seems like pleasure,
While I must remain calm.

Things begin to intensify,
Then joy explodes from inside.

Was I pleasing, or was it pleasure?

I'm relaxed now, or did I die?

I don't understand.

Daddy Is That You?

Joy, comfort, a tender touch, safety, and knowing who to trust,
Daddy, is that you?

Kind expressions, feeling reassured, believing in every word,
Daddy is that you?

Emotions begin to rise, from deep inside,
Strange lustful eyes, a familiar smell, associated with pleasure,
Daddy is that you?

All at once, passion, fear, shame, blame,
exploded in every direction,
Daddy is that you?

Confused, embarrassed, feeling dirty, mutilated, and empty,
Daddy is that you?

What Makes You Want To Do That?

What makes you want to do that?

("It's because I love you.")

People don't hurt people they love, do they?

What makes you want to do that?
("It's because you're so pretty and you smell so good")

That doesn't give you the right, does it?

What makes you want to do that?

("It feels so good!")

Not to me, it doesn't, does it?

What makes you want to do that to "ME" ?

("You're special, my favorite, and I know
you won't tell, will you!")

Deafening rage blocks out what I want to yell
every time you do that.

Incest, My Dependent Alliance

Was I daddy's precious little princess, or his love goddess?
Did I innocently see reassurance, or sinfully
clutch onto carnality?

Daddy's addiction empowered him with control,
To maneuver me through shame,
Forging my mind like steel to focus on his impure sinful acts,
Which pillaged me of my chastity.

Coerced and confused, my love torn heart concealed the truth,
To keep it near and dear, like a fragile bird,
Careful not to expose it to the elements per chance I might die.

This secret, like a vampires bite made me his possession,
A temptress, lurking by night, a zombie by day.

I continue to pray,
yet death comes not to a ghoul such as I.

This Precious Burden

Almost as if coveting, one embraces tenderly,
This precious burden.

Nurturing wholeheartedly, she continually evades inadequacy,
This precious burden.

Constantly searching and researching what would be best for,
This precious burden.

Blind eyes, cold hearts, empty of love, leaving her alone,
This precious burden.

Questions Unanswered

I don't know where it started, how it did begin,
Don't know if I should write about it, or covet it deep within.

Screams like thunder, "crash" inside my head,
Thoughts like lightening "flash" before my sight.

Where's the quiet after the storm?

Tears appear, swells begin to rise, drowning in a sea of sorrow,

Why isn't the salt burning my eyes?

My imagination isn't getting carried away,
What I'm experiencing is real and true.

Why does doubt overshadow my perception?

Disregarded feelings, avoided truths,
Might be sustaining my pain.

When this is all over, will "I" still remain?

The Confusion

She asks these questions,
The reason, I'm not sure.

The answers that I give,
I wish they could say more.

Who gives me the strength to endure?
What keeps me hopeful of tomorrow?
Why did he choose to lust me?

("I'd feel lost if he didn't.")

Where did I learn to love?
When did I learn not to cry?

("I wish I could, I wish I could.")

How do I hold on while I'm healing,
Without spiraling into an abyss?

Does Anybody Really Know?

Does anybody really know?

("How could they, you never let it show")

Afraid someone will do it again, I cleverly conceal,
hiding the pain.

Drained by resistance, feeling blotted from existence,
Broken hearted, protecting the wounds,
Scraping, painstakingly, for a little piece of me.

Time plays an important part,
Reflecting oceans of tears, for missing childhood years,
Drowning in emptiness, wondering,

Does anybody really know?

This Sticky Thing Called Pain

Like money snot, gluey pizza cheese,
This sticky thing called pain holds on.

Stuck to it, co-dependently adhered,
Resembling Siamese twins,
Fearful any attempt to separate would leave me alone,
With only death to face.

Decisions once denied me, now so piercingly thrust my way,
Terrified I'll cut my own throat.

Frustrated, anxiously seeking solutions to dissolve
the slimy mucus,
This sticky thing called pain.

Pretending To Be An Actress

What's my part, what's my line,
acting like me is all I know how to be.

What do I do?

("Pretend to be an actress")

Curtain's up, lights are on, the music's starting to play.

("That's your cue!")

The audience is waiting, the show's about to begin,

Her performance will earn spectacular reviews.

I'm not an observer without compassion,

I'm a witness; I was there, pretending to be an actress!

I'm a Dancer, I'm an Actress

Where did I begin, was it before I became me?
Were my parents my choice, did they play a part in my destiny?

Searching for myself, reflecting from within,
While grabbing onto life, through all the strife,
Hoping to learn who I am, where I'm going,
How will I get there, what will I become?

Parent's fears passed onto me, torn in many directions,
Reaching out, too far, too hard, too fast,
Losing myself in the crowd with no fear of my own.

Adrift, bobbing, bewildered, I retreated deep inside my soul,
Getting in touch with my center, a light, an eminence,
Seeking the radiance of who I really am.
A reflection of something more.

Dancing, acting, mothering, all played a part,
Each with its strings that tug at my heart.

Death reflects oceanic waves, splashing inspirations,
Metaphysically tied to life, through all that I do.

I'm a dancer, I'm an actress!

Is It She or Is It Me?

Her past was vile, it ripped off her wings!

I'm unique and proud.

She was thrown away, considered ugly and disgusting!

I'm special and distinctive.

She's useless, she's been abused; she doesn't deserve to live!

I'm creative and exceptional.

She's empty; feeling a void inside, and full of rage!

I'm gentle and sensitive.

She's out of touch with her feelings, unsure of the future,
She doesn't know if she wants to live!

I'm compassionate and optimistic.

Windows of the Heart

Cornerstones and beach front pebbles
Are all shattering to the heart.

Step back if you're barefoot,
There's glass everywhere!

Little Miss Desperado

Little Miss Desperado, was new and unknowing,
It all seemed like a natural part of her growing.

Curious to learn and so full of joy,
She was easily pleased by a simple little toy.

She strolled in the sun, down her bright sunny path,
At that time she feared nothing; except for God's wrath!

As she walked down her path one bright sunny morning,
She was suddenly snatched up, without any warning.

She was conditioned by force with coercion and threats,
At times it was like she was part of their bets.

Watching those treacherous thieves, ruthless thugs
and slimy vipers,
She soon came to realize they were really nothing like her.

She was never allowed to ask questions why,
Just to do what she's told, shut up or die.

She was taught to fear everything that came near,
And never allowed to shed a tear.

Conned by those deceivers, she lost sight of her way,
On that bright sunny path, on that bright sunny day.

She was lied to and tricked with incestual vicious pranks,
Never even given so much as a thanks.

They near killed her self-love, insisted she completely
depend on them,
Which diligently kept her wondering,
who, what, why, where and when.

They kept her busy, feelin crazy and dizzy,
far away from the now,
With no time to seek out the how, oh dear God,
what will she ever do now?

All through her pain, God kept sight of her inside desire,
As he kindled and fanned that tiny little fire.

When God saw that she could not bear any more,
He empowered her with hope, and the key to the door.

No longer a prisoner, set free by God's wrath,
Little Miss Desperado is back on her bright sunny path.

There's a Hole in My Heart

There's a hole in my heart where the rain gets in,
No one can survive the flood, not even the next of kin.

There's a hole in my heart, here comes the storm,
Quick, plug it up!

("Too Late")

There's a hole in my heart, behind the first beat, just to the left.

("Are you lost?")

There's a hole in my heart.

("What?")

There's a hole in my heart, are you deaf, or am I dead?
I don't believe you've heard a word that I've said!
Take a look inside, can you see in the dark?

("What was that?")

There's a hole in my heart, damn it!

("OK, I hear your cry, see you're in pain.")

("I'm sensitive, I care.")

("I'll help you change your attitude, build up your trust,
Rekindle the love that was lost.")

With Gods' help, we'll fill up that hold, from the inside out,
Eliminating your fears, and yourself doubt.")

("What's this? You're healing you say?")

("That's terrific, now can we go out and play?")

Eanie Meanie Minee Moe

Eanie meanie minee moe, emotions tossing to and fro,
I see you've got a great big woe, eanie meanie minee moe.

Who Gives a Damn!

Pain and fear bellow from my wretched soul,
To linger her yet another day.

Who gives a damn!

Submitting with my humble heart,
To obey until I depart.

Who gives a damn!

Death brings joy to damaged goods,
Bearing witness, the bittersweet pricks me.

Who gives a damn!

Surrounded by uncertainty, mistrust, hate and lust,
The burns are scar-less.

Who gives a damn!

Sweet, moist, tender to the touch,
Who gives a damn!

Unseen by a Loving Eye

Rain and sunshine nourish my growth,
One sees my roots run deep.

Buds continue to burst forth,
Only to whither and blow away.

Untouched by appreciation, unseen by a loving eye,
Left me barren of love once more.

Numbness of Nowhere

I walk, smile and say, "I'm feeling great"!

It's all a lie.

As truth has it,
I'm hanging on by a thin thread of faith.

In reality,
I'm hiding my pain as no one cares to know.

I'm a breath away from heaven,
An eternity away from affection,
Caught in this hallow place,
Between her and there,
The numbness of nowhere.

The Frog That Never Was

Deep in the forest, the pond was very still,
The wind was quiet and peaceful.

There amongst the lilies and cattails,
sits the frog that never was.

Keeper of the Light

Keeper of the light shining every so bright,

("Who goes there?")

Tis "I, " a shadow in the night.

("Step forward, let me see your face, tell me what you do.")

I go here and there without being seen,
Carrying messages all about your dreams.

Douse that light!, you'll reveal me, peel the paint off the wall,
Leaving no more art in sight.

("You're not making any sense, you're as high as a kite!")

No, I'm the keeper of the light."

Conception

The forbidden fruit, Adam and Eve,
"figminded" to this conception.

Intellectually cast out, Eve suddenly deceived,
Adam's heart full of lust,
Conception.

Birth renewing God's creation, so the cycle goes,
Reiteration original sin, sexual pleasure,
Conception.

Commitments, strengths and weaknesses,
Hearts beating, keeping tune with God's band,
The promise land,
Conception.

Angel Confr're

Sitting pretty, wings held high, drifting upon a cloud,
Suspended, waiting for Gods' command.

Simultaneously shifting, altering states,
Recalling the physical realm,
Pain, sadness, loneliness, despair.

Shifting gears, back to Gods' realm,
It's safe there,
Peaceful, calm, knowing nothing else compares!

Drifting in and out, yearning to stay with Him,
Keeping in touch, lifting her wings,
Embracing His love,
Angel Confr're!

Conformity Verses Transormity

To be like those who conform to the world
or become transformed,
Which shall it be?

Should I be like everybody else, just another face in the crowd?
NOT!

I'd rather hang on to my morals, and values,
Listen to God, as he speaks the truth out loud,
Give up my false strengths, overcome their defeat,
And humbly bow with love, at my dear Lords' feet.

Was This Transition?

Shaking hands, knocking knees,
Feeling extremely weak.

Discovering God, standing tall in his graces,
United in his love.

Spirit upon the rock, fears overthrown,
Strengths beyond conception.

Re-entering, succumbed with fear,
Choking, crying, wondering,
Was this transition?

Can We Go Out and Play?

Can we go play and feel the sun,
Go sing and dance and jump and run,
Enjoy it all and call it fun,
Can we go play today?

To Know the Difference

Hate, jealousy, anger, resentment, indifference, and loneliness,
To know the difference is love!

The Girls

We talk about pain lingering from long ago,
While feeling it as though it "just happened".

We share secrets we desire to shout from mountain tops,
While learning how to heal, as we struggle to survive,
At the same time questioning,
Is life with so much anguish worth living?

We encourage one another, from behind protected smiles,
Carefully guarding our shame,
Afraid of the screams that might surface,
Reminding each other of "horrors from hell".

We gently reassure one another with acceptance,
Generously giving permission to be who we are,
As we stand vigilant, defiant of defeat!

We are "The Girls" who were incested at an innocent age,
Longing to be loved as a warm sensitive women,
Healing one day at a time.

My Counselor

Feeling safe, knowing he's there, willing to help,
Greeting me at the threshold, walking the pathway,
Guiding me from the beginning,
My counselor.

Addressing unsettled issues, recalling horrifying events,
Identifying painful emotions,
Dissociating negative connections,
Exercising my weakened trust,
From a wound inflicted long ago by lust.

Understanding, patiently encouraging me to grow,
My counselor.

Teaching is the Way

A knowing, nestled within my hemispheres,
Intelligence yearning to be activated and shared.

History, questioning past events, seeking future possibilities,
Educating, and developing individual awareness.

Guiding thoughts, learning who we are, what our future holds.

I can make a difference!

Teaching is the way.

Friends of the Heart

Friends of the heart, know a tender touch,
Full armed hugs, arts to be treasured.

Masterpieces kept in a stronghold,
within the spirit forever.

I Don't Know Why

I don't know why or at what point a skirmish took the helm,
Between my daughters and I.

Leading to the emotional storm,
Creating swells so high, I fear my ship will sink.

I don't know why their rejection derails me at times,
Like raging winds out of my control.

I don't know why their angry words, fighting and blame,
Weaken the hull of my soul,
Like a ship having faced too many battles.

I don't know why dissension continues to rule our relationship,
Crashing us against the rocks, along the cliffs of our life.

I don't know why havoc continues to rule,
keeping a wedge between my daughters and I.

I don't know why.

My Loved Ones

If I were a mosquito, I'd bite them one by one,
Spreading my "joy" to my loved ones.

If I were a bee, I'd collect lots of honey,
Using it to sweeten my loved ones.

If I were a dragon fly, I'd soar high,
Collect happy molecules to sprinkle on my loved ones.

If I were an ant, I'd gather bread crumbs and
Peanut butter drops for my loved ones,
So they could have a food fight on a Saturday afternoon.

If I were a lady bug, I'd sit in their flower gardens and
think about my loved ones.

If I were a butterfly, I'd flutter my wings,
spin a cocoon around their hearts,
And metamorphosize my loved ones.

You and I

Sometimes we act silly,
While learning to discover each other,
You and I.

Taking time to absorb,
Feel the harmony in our touch,
You and I.

We're oft' times busy, creating and designing,
You and I.

Sure to hold on to who we really are,
Without losing sight of each other,
You and I.

We're enjoying love more and more,
As we do things we've never done before,
You and I.

Exercising our wings, exploring new and exciting things,
We continue to nourish our love in each other,
You and I.

My Honey and I

In the tall pines, we sit alone and sublime,
My honey and I.

We scope the blue skies and the vast forest around us,
My honey and I.

Soft winds lift our spirits, as we walk about,
My honey and I.

We coo and mate and enjoy our time together,
In the tall pines,
My honey and I.

About the Author

"Photo by Natasha Tomaselli"

That I lived to write these poems is a miracle.

Prior to the age of six, I was preconditioned to tolerate verbal, physical, emotional, mental and sexual abuse.

Before and during and after my five years of counseling, frozen cubicles of repressed anger, terror, humility, guilt, and horrifying memories surfaced.

As a way of expressing past hurts and etching toward recovery, I wrote many poems from 1991 to 2004.

I dedicate these poems to my inner child, a survivor, "Butch".

I want to thank my husband Allan for his steadfast and continued support and unconditional love. Without it, I would not have been able to heal.

These poems are subject to copyright and may not be used without my express permission.

Barbara J. Knutsen